BOOTFUL OF WINE

ALICE KING

Mandarin
in association with
Mitchell Beazley

for Bluey

A Bootful of Wine

Edited and designed by
Mitchell Beazley International Ltd
Michelin House, 81 Fulham Road
London SW3 6RB

Copyright © Mitchell Beazley International Ltd 1993
Published by Mitchell Beazley as a Mandarin paperback
Text © Alice King 1993

A CIP record for this book is available from the British Library.

ISBN 0 7493 1548 2

Executive Editor: Anne Ryland
Editor: Susan Keevil
Art Director: Tim Foster
Art Editor: Paul Drayson
Production: Sarah Schuman
Film by Tradespools Ltd, Frome, Somerset
Printed and bound in Great Britain by
Cox & Wyman, Reading
Typeset in Garamond

CONTENTS

PART ONE

PLANNING YOUR BOOTFUL

PART TWO

THE BOOTFUL OF WINE STYLE GUIDE

The Wine Regions of France

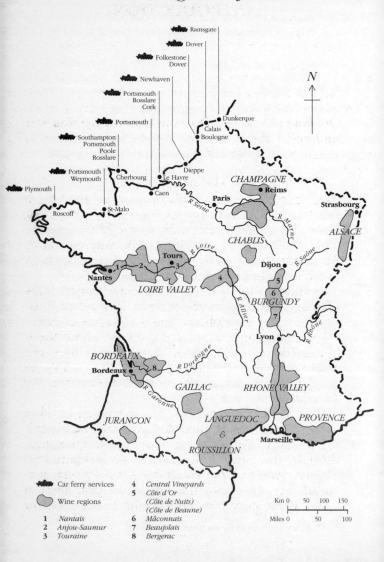

N

Ramsgate
Dover
Folkestone
Dover
Newhaven
Portsmouth
Rosslare
Cork
Portsmouth
Southampton
Portsmouth
Poole
Rosslare
Portsmouth
Weymouth
Plymouth
Roscoff
St-Malo
Cherbourg
Caen
Le Havre
Dieppe
Dunkerque
Calais
Boulogne

CHAMPAGNE
Reims
Strasbourg
R Seine
Paris
R Marne
ALSACE
CHABLIS
R Loire
Tours
Dijon
R Saône
2
3
Nantes
1
LOIRE VALLEY
4
5
6
BURGUNDY
7
R Allier
Lyon
R Rhône
BORDEAUX
8
R Dordogne
Bordeaux
GAILLAC
RHONE VALLEY
R Garonne
JURANCON
LANGUEDOC
&
ROUSSILLON
PROVENCE
Marseille

Car ferry services

Wine regions

1	*Nantais*	
2	*Anjou-Saumur*	
3	*Touraine*	
8	*Bergerac*	

4	*Central Vineyards*
5	*Côte d'Or*
	(Côte de Nuits)
	(Côte de Beaune)
6	*Mâconnais*
7	*Beaujolais*
8	*Bergerac*

Km 0   50   100   150
Miles 0   50   100

PART ONE

INTRODUCTION

Do you like wine? Do you like saving yourself money? If the answer to these two questions is yes, then *A Bootful of Wine* is the book for you.

The new deal

Now that 1993 is here, Britain and Ireland* have finally relaxed their customs controls. We can now bring home from Europe as much as 90 litres of table wine without paying any UK duty or VAT**. Alternatively, we are allowed to bring back as much as 60 litres of sparkling wine.

In addition to 90 litres of still wine (or 60 litres of sparkling) we can also import 20 litres of fortified wine, 10 litres of spirits and 110 litres of beer.

The European Commission's advice about these '*guideline*' quantities (for that is what they are called, rather than 'limits') is that they apply to goods '*carried personally by the traveller and not for commercial use*'.

This actually means that you may well be able to bring back more, provided you are not intending to sell it. For anything above these quantities, though, travellers will have to be prepared to '*demonstrate that the goods are for their own personal use*', to quote the European Commission again. Quite how you prove to the customs officer

* ** Please see page 10 for Footnotes

that you are going to throw a really large party I'm not quite sure, although I expect it can be done!

How *A Bootful of Wine* can help you

Not everyone goes to France with an empty car boot just waiting to be filled up with wine. After a holiday it is more likely the car will be packed with luggage, holiday souvenirs and children.

But whether you've only got room for just a case or two, or you have decided to make a special wine buying journey, *A Bootful of Wine* will help you choose which wines are to your taste, which you can make the best savings on, and how to get the most out of your Bootful of duty-free wine.

Ninety litres is a substantial amount, the equivalent to ten cases, or 120 average size (75cl) bottles: enough wine for hours of enjoyable drinking, but an awful lot to have hanging around if, on tasting, you discover you have made the wrong choice.

A Bootful of Wine will help avoid such unpleasant shocks. Instead, you'll be able to choose wines from the French supermarket shelves confidently, safe in the knowledge that you will enjoy them when you get back home.

To this end, the second section of the book is a great adventure. It tells you about a multitude of previously untried wines simply by grouping together those of similar styles. So if, for example, you look up an old favourite such as beaujolais, (a light- to medium-bodied red), you'll find a whole host of red wines like it in the entries alongside.

How much money can you save?

The new duty free laws will allow you to make a substantial saving on medium to lower priced wines where the duty makes up a significant proportion of the price. And while you will not have as much purchasing power as at your local super-market back home, you should still be able to buy these types of wine much more cheaply than the British supermarkets and wine merchants can because they still have to pay duty.

With UK duty currently standing at around 95 pence a bottle plus VAT (or £1.11 a bottle includ-ing VAT), you save at least £13.32 on just 12 bot-tles. The saving on sparkling wines is even greater as they attract the higher duty rate of £1.83 a bot-tle, including VAT: the saving is £21.96 for a case of 12 bottles.

Because duty is a tax on volume and not on value, the cheaper and medium priced wines are the ones where the difference will really be noticed. If, for instance, you normally spend £3 on a bottle of wine in Britain, the same bottle will be at least £1.11, or a massive 37%, cheaper in France. But a £10 bottle might still be just £1.11 cheaper, a saving of only 11%. An important point to remem-ber is that the more expensive wines are often much cheaper in Britain anyway.

At the end of the day though, by bringing back your entire allowance of 90 litres of wine it is pos-sible to save yourself a total of £133.20, in duty and also VAT on the duty.

What is in *A Bootful of Wine*?

The first part of *A Bootful of Wine* tells you much of what you need to know before buying your wine. It explains what the labels and vintages mean, what different grape varieties taste like, and how to choose the right wine for the right occasion.

Once you've bought the wine, it explains how to get the maximum safely into your car boot, how to get it back home, and then how to store it.

The second part describes over 200 wines you are likely to find on French supermarket shelves. For easy reference these are sorted into style sections, ranging from light dry whites to heavy full-bodied reds and to rosés. The sections will enable you to look up a favourite wine, Muscadet for example, and discover a whole host of similar (and often cheaper) alternatives. Price guides for each wine will help you plan your budget beforehand.

A Bootful of Wine does not aim to be a comprehensive guide to all French wines, however, but is a glance at what is most often available in the French supermarkets.

How to use A Bootful of Wine

You can use this book in several different ways. Either you can look through it before making the journey to France, and use the style guide to help you decide what sort of wines you want to buy.

Alternatively, use it as a quick reference guide while in French supermarkets or wine shops. If you come across a wine you haven't heard of, look it up in the index and cross-reference it to the entry in the style sections where it will describe what it tastes like.

Planning what kind of wine to buy
– Bootful occasions

Apart from everyday drinking, there are a number of occasions where buying a quantity of wine all at once makes a lot of sense.

Do you have any special celebrations, a party or a wedding coming up? If so, now is the time to decide what type of wine you want to drink. Do you want white or red wine, dry or sweet, sparkling or fortified? How much do you want to spend per bottle?

By looking through the entries in *A Bootful of Wine* you will be able to mark up a selection of possible wines before going over to France to see exactly what is on the shelves.

WINE FOR PARTIES
The best way to use the new duty-free allowance is for parties. As seen already, it is when you buy cheap wines that you can really save money, and, if you are making a special journey to fetch them, you can have a fun day out in one of the French Channel ports at the same time.

Suggested party wines to buy (all in the 'F' price category – *see* page 50) would be dry and medium whites, and light- to medium-bodied reds. It is also worth bringing in your beer allowance if space and weight permits as this too is so cheap in France.

WINE FOR WEDDINGS AND CHRISTENINGS
Because of the substantial saving to be made on sparkling wines, now's your chance to stock up on a few cases of fizz for your wedding or for a christening. If, for the former, you are having a decent sized reception the same comments apply as for parties (*see above*). Why not have a pre-honeymoon honeymoon and go over to France for a couple of days, staying overnight and bringing the wedding champagne and wine back the following day!

Suggested wines to buy: sparkling wine or champagne. Moderately priced red and dry to medium-dry white.

WINES FOR SPECIAL OCCASIONS, DINNER PARTIES, ETC

For a special treat, bring back some of your favourite wines, even if they are in the more expensive 'FF' to 'FFF' price ranges (*see* page 50). But make sure you have a local British supermarket or off-license's price list to hand for comparison, as the more expensive wines are often even more highly priced in France, despite there being no duty to pay.

Important Footnotes

*   Ireland's customs controls are in fact slightly less relaxed than Britain's, their 'guideline quantities' being: 45 litres for still wine, 30 litres for sparkling wine, 20 litres for fortified wine and 55 litres for beer – for spirits they are the same, 10 litres.

**   The duty free guidelines apply to goods where the duty and VAT have been paid in the country where they were purchased. This is all included in the price of wine sold in standard retail shops like supermarkets.

     Don't make the mistake of buying wine direct from producers without paying the local duty or VAT. Check that the bottles have a green '*capsule congée*' sticker on the very top; this indicates that French duty has been paid. If you are not sure about this, ask the vendor for a VAT receipt which will show their VAT registration number.

     This is important, as, if you cannot prove to British customs that you have paid French duty and VAT, you could be liable to pay it on your return to England.

CHAPTER 1

PACKING THE WINE IN

How to get the most, safely, into your car boot

So, you decide to make a special trip over to France to load up with wine for a party. In theory it all sounds very easy. You get together with three friends, pack everyone into the hatchback and whizz off to France to bring back 40 cases of duty free wine! In practice, it is less simple. There is not room for you, your three friends, and the 40 cases in the standard hatchback, or even the standard estate car.

Not everyone crossing the channel is going to want to bring back forty cases of duty free wine though. And if you are returning from your holidays you are unlikely to have an empty car unless you have disposed of both luggage and children or friends! In either instance, you may only be bringing home a small amount.

But, whether you are making a trip especially to buy wine, or are bringing back just a few cases after a holiday, there are several important safety tips to take into consideration.

To help you avoid getting into trouble with the police in France and Britain, not to mention your insurance company and your health, I had a look at several aspects requiring prior planning if you are to make the most of your Bootful of wine.

First of all, I looked at the space factor. How

many cases of wine will actually fit into the cars we drive? The answers surprised me and many of my friends. As I come from quite a large family, I examined the cars that various members of the family owned. We came up with a good cross-section: a sports car, a hatchback, a saloon, a standard estate and a large estate.

My little sports car was, predictably, the least successful by a long way – we could only fit one case of wine in the boot. My brother-in-law's saloon, a Ford Sierra, took ten cases in the boot, while my brother's VW Golf GTi, a hatchback, easily took 20 cases with the back seats down. My parents' Citröen BX estate took 35 cases, as did my sister's massive Peugeot 505 estate with three rows of seats (usually packed with children rather than wine).

As far as space is concerned then, it is possible to make some generalisations, even though car boot sizes will vary from model to model. You can expect to pack 16 to 18 cases in a small hatchback, 10 in a standard saloon boot, 20 in a standard hatchback, and 30 to 35 cases in an estate.

Remember though that these estimates are all based on just two people being in the car, with no other luggage and the back seats folded down (with the exception of the saloon). Your car is unlikely to be so clutter-free when returning from holiday.

To see how many cases you can get into your car (in terms of space), just do an experiment with a few empty wine boxes. But don't forget to make allowance for luggage and other passengers or children.

In terms of space (but not always weight, *see opposite*), roof racks can come in handy, as can trailers. But be warned; the latter will add a heavy supplement to your ferry costs.

Having determined the space available, I looked at weight. This is something many people forget about. It is essential to have an idea of the weight your car is permitted to carry both for safety's sake, as well as the law's; weight limits mean, for example, that it is unlikely that you will be able to fill an estate car completely with wine without overloading it, and if you are seen to be overloaded you could be stopped by the police.

Check your handbook (or manual) to see how much weight you are allowed to carry. This weight is referred to as the 'payload' of the car: the 'gross vehicle weight' less the 'kerb weight'. Most of the manuals I looked at were far from clear on this subject, however, so I asked some local dealers for their advice. Surprisingly, perhaps, they were not much more explicit themselves. As a last resort though, it is always possible to obtain the manufacturer's head office number from your local dealer and ask their technical department yourself for your car's exact loading specifications.

An average cardboard case of 12 bottles (each 75cl) weighs 17kgs. Finer, more expensive wines (rarely a good Bootful buy in France), which are packed in wooden cases, are much heavier at 20kgs. Sparkling wine and champagne are heavier still due to the thicker glass used for the bottles and weigh in at 21.6kgs a case. And half bottles and magnums weigh even more, again because of their extra glass.

Conversely, some of the cheapest everyday table wine is sold in litre or litre-and-a-half plastic bottles. These are light and will save on weight if you are worried about carrying too much.

When calculating the load you are able to carry

safely, don't forget to allow for the weight of your passengers too; a good average to take is 75kgs per person.

Using a Golf GTi as an example, space-wise you can fit in 20 plus cases. The payload is 515kgs so, deducting 150kg for two people (driver and passenger), you can actually load 365kgs. Divide this by 17kgs (the weight of a case of wine) and you have 21 cases in total. In this example the permitted weight and space available happen to allow for roughly the same quantity. But there is no guarantee that this will always be the case, so it is important check it out first.

Certain cars, particularly estate cars and jeeps, contain a plate, often located in the engine compartment, which states the maximum weight of loading and towing. If your weight exceeds this limit you could be stopped by the police and prosecuted.

You don't have to be a mathematician, however, to decide whether your car is overloaded or unsafe to drive. If the wheel flaps are dragging on the floor, the exhaust trailing along the ground, the suspension sagging, and/or the car looks unstable, the police are likely to pull you over. This could result in your being charged for driving your car in a 'dangerous condition', which could leave a sour taste in your mouth, not to mention its mark on your wallet and driving license.

To help ensure you get your liquid Bootful home safely, take note of the following safety tips, devised in conjunction with the RAC especially for this book.

(1) Before packing your Bootful, check your car handbook to find out its payload. Don't overload your car or you are likely to be stopped.

(2) Try to get an even distribution with the bulk of the weight over or between the wheels. If involved in an accident while overloaded, or loaded carelessly, you may well find you are not covered by your insurance.

(3) It's safer and more practical (especially once you reach the end of your journey) to transport your wine in cases. Loose bottles can be a smashing liability, particularly if you have to brake suddenly.

(4) When loading the car, remember not to obstruct your rear-view mirror.

(5) Once loaded, check your stopping distances: braking takes much longer in a loaded car.

(6) Check the steering. Again, this alters when your car is loaded.

(7) Once full, check your tyre pressure; this needs regular attention when carrying a heavy weight. Pressures for carrying a full load will be detailed in your manual.

(8) Make sure the cases are well secured, otherwise taking a tight corner could result in smashed bottles.

(9) Take a rug to cover the cases if you have to stop overnight on the way home. This will discourage car thieves from helping themselves to some of your liquid assets.

(10) Although it is not recommended to carry

cases on a roof-rack, if you must, make sure they are covered with polythene, otherwise, in heavy rain the cardboard boxes could disintegrate – you will then begin to shed your load!

(11) You must have with you a valid full driving license, vehicle registration documents (if you are driving a company car you need a letter authorising you to use it) and a warning triangle or hazard warning lights. Legally in France you must also display a GB sign.

(12) In France each passenger must have a fixed seat and children under the age of ten are not allowed to sit in the front of the car. You must also remember to wear your seat belt.

(13) Finally, and very importantly if you are driving, NEVER take the risk of sampling your Bootful purchases before reaching home.

CHAPTER 2

UNDERSTANDING THE LABEL

Stop right here! Don't flip on to the next chapter!

Bottle shapes

How can you tell what a wine is likely to taste like before even drawing the cork? Apart from the wealth of information on the label (*see* further on in this chapter) you can deduce a certain amount from the actual shape of the bottle. And while it is always dangerous to generalise as there are many exceptions, this clairvoyant way of choosing wine can be very helpful – if only in that it gives you a guideline before studying the label of your chosen bottle in more depth.

THE BORDEAUX BOTTLE
This has straight sides with indented shoulders. It is most often seen containing red wines which are often a similar weight to claret, in other words medium- to full-bodied. Wines made from Bordeaux-type grape varieties like Cabernet Sauvignon and Merlot are nearly always found in this shaped bottle. Other wines you are likely to see include Fitou, Corbières, Minervois and many similar style *vins de pays*.

The Bordeaux bottle is also the classic shape for both the dry white wines of Bordeaux and the sweet ones such as Sauternes and Barsac. The giveaway sign for the sweet whites is that the bottles are nearly always made of clear glass (the wines tending to be yellow in colour), while the drier wines generally come in green bottles.

Many other Sauvignon-based dry whites from elsewhere in France are found in the Bordeaux-shaped bottles too, and tend to be of light to medium weight.

THE BURGUNDY BOTTLE

Fatter than the Bordeaux bottle, with gradually sloping shoulders, this is the shape used for all Burgundy's wines, whether they are white or red. And white wines from elsewhere made from the Chardonnay grape, Burgundy's traditional white wine variety, are generally all found in this shape of bottle too.

Loire Valley whites like Sancerre or Touraine Sauvignon are also similarly packaged, and, though made from a different grape variety (Sauvignon Blanc), are not dissimilar in weight, tending towards medium-bodied.

Rhône reds will be found in the burgundy-shaped bottle too, as will many wines made from grapes like Syrah, Grenache and Mourvèdre. These wines tend to be much fuller in style than most red burgundies.

Loire Valley reds such as Chinon and Bourgueil – more medium-bodied wines – can also be added to this list; as can beaujolais, along with Gamay and other wines grown outside the area in regions like the Ardèche.

As a general guideline, a red *vin de pays* in a burgundy-shaped bottle is likely to be lighter than one in a Bordeaux bottle.

THE CHAMPAGNE BOTTLE
This is easy to spot, due to both the bottle shape and the distinctive foil covered and wire-muzzled cork. The champagne bottle is like the burgundy bottle, but with the addition of a lip at the top of the neck. It is made from much denser, stronger glass so as to withstand the pressure of sparkling wine. All champagnes and sparkling wines come in this sort of bottle and either have champagne-style corks or – for cheaper wines – similarly shaped stoppers made of plastic.

THE ALSACE FLUTE-SHAPED BOTTLE
Tall and slim with steeply sloping shoulders, this looks rather like a classic German wine bottle but is actually slightly taller. Traditionally used for both the red and white wines of Alsace, this shape is occasionally used by winemakers from other regions too: notably sweet Muscat producers from Beaumes-de-Venise in the Rhône Valley.

THE PICHET OR SKITTLE SHAPE
This type of bottle is traditionally used for the excellent, if sometimes pricey, dry Provence rosé wines, and is made from clear glass.

Georges Duboeuf of Beaujolais fame also uses this shape for some of his prestige red wines.

Understanding the label

Being able to decipher the blurb on a French wine label will help ensure that you enjoy the wines in your Bootful. It will also make choosing from the myriad of wines available on the French supermarket shelves much easier.

Don't be put off by confusing looking labels. By understanding just a few of the terms used you will soon have a good idea of what the wine tastes like without actually having to buy it and open the bottle to find out.

The various different quality levels, explained here, are a good place to start. While 'table wines' can come from anywhere in France, all the higher quality levels will include the name of the region in which the wines were produced. Increasingly, wines will also name the grape variety (or varieties) from which they were made on their labels, and some will mention whether the wine is dry, sweet, or made in an unusual way which has changed the flavour (oak-aged for example).

Listed after the quality definitions below are the majority of terms you are likely to come across.

Legal quality definitions in France

VIN DE TABLE

This is basic table wine that can come from any region of France. There are no quality controls and grapes can come from any region.

Vins de tables can be good, bad or indifferent, depending upon the producer. All are sold under different brand names throughout the EC, and, in general, there are many much better value and more consistent wines to be bought for the Bootful.

Indeed, for just a few francs a bottle more (or sometimes even less if you are comparing it to a well-known branded table wine), you can get a quality *vin de pays* or an *appellation contrôlée* wine and feel much more confident about the quality. Because of this, *vins de tables* are not included in *A Bootful of Wine*.

VIN DE PAYS
This is wine from a designated region of France, with quality controls that are less strict than those for *appellation contrôlée* wines (*see below*). There are currently over 140 regions which are entitled to label their wines '*vin de pays*'.

The range of these wines available in supermarkets will vary greatly from region to region. Though noticeable in British supermarkets, the price difference between *vins de pays* and *appellation contrôlée* wines is much less marked in France.

VIN DÉLIMITÉ DE QUALITÉ SUPÉRIEURE (VDQS)
This is a quality level that falls in between *vin de pays* and *appellation contrôlée*. The wines come from designated regions, many of which are gradually being upgraded to *appellation contrôlée* status; once this happens their produce immediately becomes more expensive!

APPELLATION D'ORIGINE CONTROLÉE
(AOC *or* AC)
The highest quality French wines. '*Appellation contrôlée*' applies to specific regions and defines strictly controlled, permitted grape varieties and yields. Many larger ACs (eg, AC Bordeaux or AC Bourgogne) include other smaller (and higher quality) ACs.

In French supermarkets, the price differential between cheaper appellation wines and table wines is far less than in Britain. While there are still good and less good AC wines, the extra quality guarantee is often worth paying a few extra francs for.

It can sometimes, though, be more helpful to follow a producer than an appellation. For example, a good producer's AC Bourgogne may be better than another producer's more expensive, and theoretically higher quality, AC Pommard (the latter a much smaller, more specialised AC within Bourgogne). This is why it is worth noting the producer or château name of any wines you particularly enjoy; also those you dislike so you can avoid them next time.

How to find your way around a French wine label

The following is a glossary of the terms you are most likely to come across on the labels of French wines:

Barriques neuves – New oak barrels.

Blanc – White.

Blanc de Blancs – White wine made from white grapes.

Blanc de Noirs – White wine made from black grapes.

Bouteille – Bottle.

Brut – Dry.

Cépage – Grape variety.

Chai – Cellar.

Château – Wine estate, especially in Bordeaux.

Clos – Walled vineyard.

Coopérative – Wine growers' cooperative.

Crémant – Sparkling, but not as frothy as champagne.

Cru – A vineyard or 'growth'.

Cru Classé – 'Classed growth'; a highly classified vineyard, especially in Bordeaux.

Cuve – A vat; sometimes indicates a better wine.

Cuve Close – Sparkling wine made in tanks (not

as good as *méthode champenoise*).

Cuvée – Contents of a vat; usually a better wine
  if included in the wine name.

Demi-Sec – Medium dry/Medium sweet.

Domaine – Estate.

Doux – Sweet.

Elevé – Matured.

Embouteilleur – Bottler.

Futs de Chêne – Oak barrels.

Grand Vin – A château's main wine (some châteaux
  make two wines).

Grand Cru – In Burgundy, a specific definition for
  top vineyards. Elsewhere, it can mean anything!

Liquoreux – Sweet.

Mas – Estate (especially in southern France).

Méthode Champenoise – Sparkling wine made in
  the same way as champagne.

Millésime – Vintage.

Mis en bouteille au château/domaine – Estate
  bottled.

Mis en bouteille de nos caves – Bottled in our cellars.

Mis en bouteille par... – Bottled by...

Moelleux – Sweet.

Mousseux – Sparkling or frothy.

Négociant – A merchant who trades in wine.

Négociant-Eleveur – As above, but who produces
  wine too.

Nouveau – New; generally wine of the latest vintage.

Off-dry – Medium dry to medium sweet.

Perlé – Lightly sparkling.

Pétillant – Wine with a very slight natural sparkle.

Pièce – Oak barrel.

Primeur – The new wine from the latest vintage.

Premier Cru – 'First Growth'; the top rank of
  Bordeaux châteaux, the second rank to Grand
  Cru in Burgundy.

Produit de l'Agriculture Biologique – Organically produced.

Rouge – Red.

Rosé – Rosé.

Sec – Dry.

Société – Company (as in Limited Company).

Sur Lie (or *Tiré sur Lie*) – Wine bottled straight from its lees (the natural yeast sediment left after fermentation).

Vendange Tardive – Wines made from grapes which are picked late in the season; sweet wines.

Vieillissement en... – Aged in... (eg, oak barrels).

Vin Ordinaire – Table wine.

Vin Tranquille – Still wine.

Vignoble – Vineyard.

Vin de Garde – A wine to lay down/mature.

Vin de Table – Table wine.

Pronouncing wine names

If you are worried about trying to pronounce the names of certain wines, don't be. Each wine name in the style section of this book (Part Two) is also shown phonetically, the way it sounds.

Tasting terms used

In *A Bootful of Wine* I have tried to steer clear of 'winespeak'. But there are times when the only way to describe a wine or its flavour is to use more technical descriptions. These are explained below.

Acidic – Acid is found naturally in grapes; in wine it is detected as the sharp sensation at the edge of your tongue.

Aftertaste – The flavour left in the mouth after swallowing a wine.

Aroma – The smell of the wine.

Body – The density of the wine.
Bootful Wine – One worth buying for your Boot!
Bottle-Age – How long the wine has been in bottle.
Bouquet – The smell of the wine.
Depth – The flavour complexity of the wine.
Earthy – Dry, coarse (but attractive) texture.
Farmyardy – Smells like a farmyard does!
Finish – The taste which remains in the mouth after the wine has been swallowed.
Fruit – The integral flavour of the grape.
Full – A wine with mouth-filling fruit.
Full-bodied – Mouth-filling wine with lots of fruit and tannin.
Grassy – Like the smell of freshly-cut grass.
Hard – Acidic wine with harsh-flavoured fruit and lots of bitter tannin.
Long – Wine with flavours that last for a long time in the mouth after swallowing.
Mousse – The amount and consistency of the bubbles in a sparkling wine.
Nose – The smell of the wine.
Oaky – A flavour of the oak barrels in which some wine is matured.
Oxidised – When the wine has come into contact with too much oxygen and tastes like vinegar.
Palate – The wine's taste.
Rich – Luscious wine.
Round – Wine with a smooth fruit flavour.
Short – Used to describe a wine with little or no aftertaste.
Spritz – Wine with a slight sparkle; just a prickle on the tongue.
Tannin – A bitter substance also found in tea and coffee. It gives the wine body and structure, and the ability to last for many years.
Vinification – The way the wine is made.

CHAPTER 3

VINTAGES

You might well have heard that the vintage, or the year in which a wine was made, is very important. It can be, especially for the top wines like Bordeaux or burgundy which are grown in marginal climates (on the climatic edge of the area where grapes will ripen).

But the vintage is of little importance for many everyday-drinking wines – especially those made in the southern part of France where the weather is constantly warm, producing grapes of consistent quality. Mostly these wines are made for drinking young anyway, a good few of them being real Bootful bargains.

However, the following general guidelines, given in the same order as the style sections of this book, will stand you in good stead.

SPARKLING WINES
The vintage is of very little importance. Most sparkling wines are non-vintage (a blend of wines from several years). Champagne normally only carries a vintage if it is an especially good one.

LIGHT DRY WHITES
These are designed to be drunk as fresh and as young as possible, so always go for the most recent vintage.

FULL-BODIED DRY WHITES
It is only with the most expensive (and not really Bootful) wines that the vintage really matters. White burgundy, for example, is particularly good from the following vintages: 1983, 1985, 1986, 1988, 1989, 1990 and 1991.

MEDIUM-DRY AND SPICY WHITES
Most vintages of the last four years are safe, but avoid 1987 – the wines will now be tired. If you are looking for Vendange Tardive wines (the super-sweet ones) any vintage is safe as they are only made in exceptionally hot – and therefore good – years.

SWEET WHITES
Because of their high natural sugar level, these wines deteriorate very slowly, and so, unless they are more than 5 years old, their vintage is of little importance. However, there has recently been a bonanza of outstanding years in the major quality sweet white producing areas of France: 1988, 1989 and 1990 are terrific vintages for Sauternes, Barsac, and wines from the Loire like Vouvray and Coteaux du Layon.

LIGHT REDS
These are designed to be drunk young, so go for the most recent vintage: 1988, 1989, 1990 and 1991 all produced very enjoyable wines in most parts of France.

MEDIUM-BODIED REDS
As with light reds, the last four years (1988, 1989, 1990 and 1991) have all produced attractive wines in most French wine regions. For the top quality

wines like those from Bordeaux, Burgundy and the Rhône Valley, older vintages worth looking out for include 1982 (but not for burgundy), 1983, 1985 and 1986.

FULL-BODIED REDS

Full reds are often so powerful that they override weak years. A good example is the 1987 vintage. There was a lot of rain and dilution of the grape juice, yet there are some delicious Bordeaux and Rhône wines to be bought from this year, and because the vintage is unfashionable, the prices are low. So-called 'off' vintages like this, if cheap enough, sound, are certainly Bootful material. The best recent vintages include 1985, 1986, 1988, 1989 and 1990.

ROSÉS

Like light dry whites, these are made to be drunk as fresh and as young as possible, so always opt for the most recent vintage you can find.

CHAPTER 4

GRAPE VARIETIES

The best way of working out the style of wine you will enjoy is first to decide on the grape varieties that you like. You can then follow these grapes through the various regions and find wines they make with the same family characteristics.

With some wines this is made very easy as the grape variety is printed clearly on the main label; others, if you look carefully, will list the variety on the back.

Many, though, are less helpful. Most burgundy producers, for example, think that the whole world knows all white burgundy is made from the Chardonnay grape and all red from the Pinot Noir. Because of this they wouldn't dream of stating the variety on the label. It is not just the Burgundians that make this assumption. Makers of the great wines of the northern Rhône – Hermitage, Cornas, Côte-Rôtie, etc – take it for granted that you know their wines are made from the spicy Syrah; and Bordeaux has always been made from a mixture of up to four different grapes – it is assumed that you know what they are!

So every time you find a wine you haven't come across before, look it up in the index. This will lead you to its entry in a style section, which in turn will detail the grape variety or varieties it is made from. Then flick back to this chapter and read about the character of the grape in question and see if you think it is likely to be to your taste.

The basic characteristics of the grape variety will stay the same, but a wine will also reflect the region in which it is grown, as well the individual winemakers' techniques. So don't expect all wines made from the same grape variety to taste identical, they won't, though they will share similar family traits.

Not all wines are made from single grape varieties, however, and it is a misconception that one made from a blend of grapes is in any way inferior. In fact, two of France's most sought-after traditional wines, champagne and red Bordeaux, known as claret, are made from blends. Often such combinations simply depend on which grapes have been historically grown in a region, and which blends the locals, over the years, have decided produce the best results.

White wine grape varieties

Some people mistakenly think that all white wines taste the same. But it is in fact their sheer variety of flavours that makes them such an attractive proposition. White grapes produce wines of every character from light dry, through to rich, luscious and sticky sweet, and everything in between.

In many ways white grapes are more versatile than reds, as the same grape can produce both dry and sweet wines depending on their ripeness and degree of natural sugar. Chenin Blanc, for instance, grown in the Loire Valley, can produce both light dry Vouvray, and rich, deep golden, sweet Vouvray.

The range of colours produced from white grape varieties is impressive too. Every shade of yellow from an almost colourless liquid, through to lime-green tinted, lemon, and to golden yellow with amber tinges. The difference in colour is a result of the variations in thickness and pigment of the grape skins, the grape's ripeness, and the way in which the wine is made. So while a grape like Muscadet produces lightly coloured wine, Sémillon or Sauvignon produced in Sauternes in a hot vintage and then affected by noble rot, will produce a deep golden one.

As a general rule, sweet whites tend to be deeper in colour than dry whites. In addition, a white wine which has been aged in oak barrels will be more golden than one which hasn't.

Read through the following white grapes' vital statistics and make a note of those whose characteristics sound appealing.

CHARDONNAY
Still the wine world's favourite white wine grape. It is California, and more recently Australia, that have publicised this variety's undoubted star quality, although the French, keeping it quiet, have been growing this grape for centuries.

All white burgundy, from Corton-Charlemagne to Mâcon, as well as Chablis, is made from Chardonnay, but growers simply haven't thought to tell us this, mistakenly assuming that everyone already knows.

An important reason for this grape's star rating is its adaptability – it can be grown in many different soils and microclimates and the wine made by all manor of different vinification techniques. The results: a huge variety of wine styles, all with distinctive family resemblances.

Chardonnay naturally produces medium- to full-bodied white wines with an aroma of whitecurrants and with good acidity and lots of zippy but reasonably weighty, slightly limey, often buttery, fruit. When aged in oak, the grape's amazing versatility becomes apparent as it reveals rich, buttery, slightly hazelnutty bouquets and creamy, toasted, vanilla-like flavours and aftertastes.

These two styles (oak-aged and not) are very distinctive, though French labels are rarely helpful in highlighting which you are buying. '*Vieillissement* (*vieilli* or *elevé*) *en futs de chêne*' indicates that the wine has been aged in oak barrels and means that it will be of the full-bodied, rich, buttery variety, typified by more expensive white burgundies.

Other areas where Chardonnay is grown include the Loire Valley and, increasingly, areas in the south of France such as the Ardèche and the Aude. These two regions tend to produce the lighter-bodied styles.

CHENIN BLANC

One of the main grape varieties grown in the Loire Valley, Chenin Blanc has a chameleon-like versatility. It is capable of producing earthy dry whites and honeyed rich sweet dessert wines. For instance, it is responsible for both the dry and sweet wines of Vouvray, and the dry and sparkling wines of Saumur.

The dry wines have a characteristic slightly earthy, flowery aroma, with a coarse, almost honeysuckle-like fruit flavour.

The richer, sweeter wines are made from grapes which have been left longer on the vines to ripen, and so their sugar content is much higher. Rich and luscious on both the nose and palate, they have an added nuance of ripe peaches, and are sweet, yet, because of a tang of acidity, are not cloying.

GEWURZTRAMINER

France's spiciest grape variety, this is one you'll either love or hate. Grown almost exclusively in the Alsace region, Gewurztraminer makes medium- to full-bodied wines, varying from off-dry to very rich and sweet.

It has an extraordinarily pungent aroma of tropical fruits and flowers, all of which are repeated in the flavour, along with an added touch of spiciness.

Though the aroma suggests a sweet wine, most Gewurztraminers are fruity and dry with a citrus-like tang of acidity. But because of their wonderfully exotic flavours, they appear nothing like as dry as, say, a Muscadet or a Chablis.

The rich, sweeter Gewurztraminers (called Vendanges Tardives, meaning 'late harvest') are those made from grapes which have undergone an extended ripening period and have been bought in long after the normal harvest is finished. As a result their natural sugars have become very concentrated, and they make rich, spicy-sweet, tropical flavoured and quite intoxicating wines.

MUSCADET

This grape produces the bone dry, acidic wines of the same name, produced in the Pays Nantais, where the Loire river flows into the Atlantic Ocean. It has a fairly neutral aroma and dry, acidic fruit on the palate. It is also known as 'Melon de Bourgogne'.

MUSCAT

At last, a grape which actually smells of grapes when it is made into wine! The grapiest grape of all, Muscat also has an aroma of roses and jasmine. On the palate the grapey flavour is enhanced by rich, currant, almost marmalade-like undertones.

Muscat can make medium-bodied wines which finish off-dry on the palate (those from Alsace, for instance), but in France it is better known for those it produces which are rich and sticky sweet. While Muscat de Beaumes-de-Venise is the best known (and the most expensive) there are many other much better value sweet Muscats made in the south of France. Traditionally these are made even more potent by fortification with alcohol (as is Beaumes-de-Venise), and often have alcohol contents not dissimilar to port's.

The Muscat grape is also used for some sparkling wines such as Clairette de Die.

SAUVIGNON BLANC
Green, grassy and racy are appropriate descriptions for this grape variety, which makes both light- and medium-bodied dry white wines. It is a grape with a distinctive aroma of gooseberries and freshly cut green grass (some even say cat's pee!), and has a slightly smokey/flinty character which is particularly marked in the Loire Valley wines it is most famous for, Sancerre and Pouilly Fumé, as well as those from the Touraine region.

Sauvignon Blanc is also grown widely in Bordeaux and its neighbouring regions, Côtes de Duras and Bergerac for example. Here it is mixed with Sémillon to make both the dry white wines of Graves, and the rich, luscious sweet wines of Sauternes.

SÉMILLON
An underrated grape, grown mainly in the Bordeaux region where it is mixed with Sauvignon

Blanc to make dry white Graves and dessert wines from Sauternes. On its own, it produces medium- to full-bodied wines which have ripe, fruity, peachy flavours and a lanolin-like texture.

Red wine grape varieties

Many people do not know that a quality black grape has clear juice. If you cut one of these grapes in half, you will see its flesh is white. So how come the wine produced is red or purple?

Red wine's colour comes from the pigment found in the grape skins, released once the grapes have been crushed. As their juice ferments into wine, natural sugar is transformed into alcohol and bubbles of carbon dioxide. These bubbles push the skins to the top of the fermentation vats form- ing a cap (or '*chapeau*').

If a winemaker wants to extract the maximum colour from the grape skins, he will pump the wine over this cap to free as many colour pigments as possible; by doing this he will also release more tannin and flavour compounds to make a rich, full-bodied wine.

With rosé and lighter reds, the opposite effect is desired: the juice is sometimes only left in contact with the skins for a matter of hours before being drained off. This produces wines which are much more delicate in colour and flavour.

CABERNET SAUVIGNON
If you are at all sceptical about descriptions of wines' aromas which compare them to various fruits, Cabernet Sauvignon wines are the ones to change your mind. In their purest, most youthful form they really do smell of blackcurrants, often with a slightly minty, eucalyptus or green pepper edge!

The Cabernet Sauvignon grape produces medium- to full-bodied reds which have lots of fruit, but are dry with good, balancing tannin (the bitter substance found in tea and coffee). When they are more mature, especially if they have been aged in small oak barrels (as most top Bordeaux are), these wines can take on a slightly sweet aroma of tobacco, mixed with vanilla and cinnamon.

Long before the advent of the now popular Bulgarian Cabernet Sauvignon, most people will have tasted this red grape without knowing it as it forms the backbone of the Englishman's traditional tipple, claret, or red Bordeaux. In this wine it shows its true versatility, mixing perfectly with two other grape varieties, Cabernet Franc and Merlot. Indeed, it is in the company of others that it achieves its greatest heights.

Recognising Cabernet Sauvignon's potential as a quality red wine producer, growers elsewhere in France have recently taken to planting it too, particularly in the south (Provence, Oc and Ardèche) where its presence in blends adds weight and complexity.

CABERNET FRANC

This is a cousin of Cabernet Sauvignon, sharing some of the same personality traits without ever achieving quite the same peaks of greatness. Cabernet Franc produces wines with an aroma of mixed red and black berries, an earthy, grassy flavour, and a pleasant tang of acidity. It is much less bitter than the tannic Cabernet Sauvignon grape and so the wines are enjoyable to drink when much younger.

In St-Emilion and Pomerol, two major areas of Bordeaux, it is combined with Merlot, making up a more important part of this traditional blend than does Cabernet Sauvignon.

Its Loire Valley manifestations include many of the delicious medium weight red wines like Bourgueil, Chinon and Saumur-Champigny. Fruity, refreshing and very gulpable while still young, Cabernet Franc wines can also age well too.

CARIGNAN

This is the traditional grape variety of France's Pyrénées-Orientales region (just north of the Pyrenees mountains), and has more recently spread to the southern Midi.

The wines it produces are deep in colour and have lots of plummy fruit and bitter tannin. Carignan is an excellent blending grape variety, often mixed with Grenache, Cinsaut and Mourvèdre to make some of the best bargain Bootful reds in the south of France.

CINSAUT (*sometimes spelt* CINSAULT)

This is popular with growers in the south of France as it has a plentiful yield. The resulting wines can be anything from rosé through to inky black in colour, with a rustic, fruity flavour. It is rarely used on its own, but is an excellent blending grape, often teamed up with Mourvèdre (which has more tannin) and Grenache.

It forms the backbone of many of the bargain *vins de pays* of the Languedoc-Roussillon region and is often a part of the wines from the Aude, Gard and Hérault vineyards.

GAMAY

This is the archetypal fruity grape, producing wonderfully gulpable wines, bursting with ultra-juicy fruit. The Gamay grape has a relatively thin skin, and therefore it does not produce wines with great amounts of bitter, astringent tannin.

It is the grape of beaujolais fame and, when vinified in a particular way (by carbonic maceration), makes wines which actually smell like bubble-gum. Like this favourite childrens' sweet, they are fun wines, designed for easy, early drinking.

As well as in Beaujolais, it is also grown in the Loire Valley and the south of France in areas like the Ardèche. From these regions Gamay wines are high in acidity and fruit flavour, and are appealingly zippy and refreshing.

Because the majority of wines made from this grape are relatively light, drinkers who generally dislike red wine will often enjoy them. Gamay wines also take well to being served chilled. A must for everyday drinking and great for the Bootful.

GRENACHE

Widely grown throughout the southern Rhône Valley, this grape, together with its more majestic brother, Syrah, is an essential base for many of the southern Rhône wines like Châteauneuf-du-Pape and Côtes du Ventoux, as well as good old Côtes du Rhône. It is also widely grown throughout the south of France and is an essential component of many of the better red and rosé *vins de pays* and appellation wines, especially in the Languedoc-Roussillon region and throughout Provence.

Grenache itself makes relatively light wine with little tannin, which is why it is so suitable for mixing with heavier, more full-bodied southern grapes. It has lots of upfront fruit flavour of its own too, making it a delight for the wine drinker, and at the same time a pleasure for vignerons to grow as it is healthy and high yielding.

MERLOT

An impressive black grape capable of producing full-bodied, tannic, yet velvety red wines for long keeping, as well as up-front fruity wines for easy drinking. It has an attractive, plum-like, brambly aroma – which often reminds me of parma violet sweets – and lots of black plum flavour on the palate.

Merlot is one of the three main grape varieties in claret (red Bordeaux), blended with Cabernet Sauvignon and Cabernet Franc. It is the dominant part of the blend in the Libournais area (St-Emilion, Pomerol, and their outlying communes). And Pomerol's Château Pétrus, producing the world's most expensive wine, uses 95% Merlot in its blend. Wines based on Merlot are softer in character than those of Cabernet Sauvignon and are usually ready to drink when slightly younger.

Recently, it has been increasingly used on its own to make a single variety wine, and in the southwest of France is being used to produce many Bordeaux taste-alikes. Some very good examples are coming out of areas like the Oc.

MOURVEDRE

Widely planted throughout the Rhône Valley and the south of France, this is a quality blending grape for red wines. It forms the backbone of many of the best from the southern Rhône, like Châteauneuf-du-Pape, and is largely responsible for the delicious plummy wines from Provence. Many of the bargain *vins de pays* from *départements* like the Var are made from this grape.

High in acidity and tannin, it is often blended

with Grenache – much lighter, and lower in tannin – and also with Cinsaut. These three grapes are responsible for many of the bargain Bootful wines from the south of France.

PINOT MEUNIER

Widely grown in the Champagne region where it is blended with Pinot Noir and Chardonnay, Pinot Meunier is said to add fruit and body to the wines: a good bolstering grape. It is rarely found elsewhere in France and never appears on labels as a single grape variety.

PINOT NOIR

This grape variety produces some of France's most sensuous and sensational red wines: the famous red burgundies. And luckily for Burgundian wine growers (but unluckily for the rest of us) it is a notoriously difficult grape variety to grow, rarely being found outside Burgundy itself.

Pinot Noir produces wines that are lighter in colour and body than the equally famous Cabernet Sauvignon, and, at their best, reveal delicate aromas of raspberries, strawberries, straw and farmyards, with soft, lightly spicy, vanilla overtones. When the wine has been aged in new oak barrels the vanilla characteristics become even more marked and creamy.

Because of its subtlety and complexity, Pinot Noir is used as a single variety in Burgundy, having enough class and balance not to need the influence or help of any other grape.

One other main area of Pinot Noir production in France is the northern appellation of Champagne. Here it is one of three grape varieties used in the production of this region's famous wine; its colour-giving skins are removed directly after pressing so that the juice remains white.

It is also grown in the northern region of Alsace, where it features as the only major red grape variety. Here it produces wines which are normally dark rosé in colour, not as soft, velvety and complex as those produced in Burgundy, but which still retain the characteristic red fruit aromas.

Pinot Noir is grown in few other regions of France, but one where it can produce delicious, light, unusual reds is Sancerre.

SYRAH

One of France's most powerful and majestic grape varieties, Syrah is capable of producing full-bodied, inky black wines with masses of vigorous spicy fruit. They are tannic too, and have a distinctive aroma mixed with a rich, almost gamey, flavour.

Widely grown throughout the Rhône Valley, especially the northern part, this is the grape of Hermitage fame, known for its ability to produce wines which can even outlive their makers! It is also grown extensively in the hotter south of France where higher yields and different soils lead to scaled down versions: plummy and lightly spicy, with good fruit but not too much tannin.

Both used on its own and in blends, this is a characterful, earthy sort of red, a particularly interesting one to follow around different areas. Look out for single varietal *vins de pays* made from Syrah, they are great Bootful bargains.

CHAPTER 5

HOW TO STORE THE WINE ONCE BACK HOME

Once you've got your 90 litres safely back home, where do you put them? Few people live in houses with real cellars, so you need to decide where your newly imported wine is going to live. A little thought prior to going to France on your Bootful trip will pay dividends as preparing some storage space beforehand can spare you the aggravation of tripping over bottles in the hallway for weeks.

The longer you intend to keep the wine, the more important storage conditions become. Wine for fairly immediate drinking will not come to much harm kept in a wine rack, even in the warmth of the kitchen. But few of us can drink 90 litres that quickly (unless we are having a party), so here are some basic guidelines to follow.

(1) Ensure all bottles are stored lying on their sides; this way the wine keeps the cork moist, preventing it from drying out and shrinking, and thus letting oxygen in and turning the wine into vinegar.

(2) Lie the bottles down labels uppermost. Then, if the wine does contain any sediment, it will settle along the underside of the bottle. This makes decanting much easier as the sediment

is easily visible in a neat line unhidden by the label.

(3) A constant temperature is more important than a particularly cold one. The ideal cellar temperature is around 13°C (55°F).

(4) Bottles keep better if stored in the dark rather than in the light as sunlight can oxidise the wine.

(5) A spare room (perhaps under the bed or in a wardrobe) can be ideal for storage, especially if you can turn the heating off. Alternatively, a cupboard, the space under the stairs, a garden shed or the garage can be put to good use. It is always best to find a north-facing room or shed, as this receives less direct sunlight in the summer, helping keep the temperatures down.

(6) Organise your wine in whatever seems the most practical way to you. This could be by style (following the style categories in Part Two of *A Bootful of Wine*), putting all light reds together, for example; or by region perhaps, with all the Loire wines together.

Alternatively, you could arrange them by price, separating them into everyday drinking wines and more expensive wines intended for special occasions.

(7) It's a good idea to keep a list of when you bought the wines, where and for how much. That way they are easier to trace if you want to buy some more.

How long do wines keep?

Both in the bottle, and once opened, this can depend on how long you can resist drinking them! It also depends on the quality and colour of the wine. There's one very obvious indicator of a wine' maturity that many people forget, and that's the bottle size. Wine matures much faster in half bottles than in standard bottles, so these should be kept for a shorter time. Conversely, large bottles, especially of medium- to full-bodied reds, mature more slowly. These rules, however, do not really apply to cheap table wines, which should always be drunk young.

Vins de tables (table wines) should be drunk within six months of purchase, and as whites deteriorate faster than reds, you'll really get the best out of them by drinking them as young as possible. Some red table wines will last longer, but it's not worth pushing your luck by keeping them for more than a year. Don't leave bottles of either colour open for more than a few hours.

White *vins de pays* are similar, although the slightly heavier ones may stay fresh for up to a year. Again, though, it's not a good idea to keep whites for more than a few hours once opened. Fuller-bodied red *vins de pays* can keep for up to five years, and the heavier ones will survive for up to 24 hours once opened.

With *appellation contrôlée* wines it is more difficult to generalise on lifespan and on keeping once opened as there is such a great quality range.

Keeping opened bottles of wine is easier if you remember a few simple rules:

(1) Wine will always keep better in an opened bottle when at a lower temperature, so putting

it in the fridge will help a lot.

(2) Always shove the cork back in (the same way it was when you opened the bottle).

(3) It can help to decant the wine into a smaller (clean) bottle. Mixer bottles are ideal.

(4) The heavier the red, the longer it can last once opened.

But, remember, you will almost always get the most out of a wine by sharing it with friends and drinking the whole bottle at one sitting.

Here's a rough guide to keeping your wines, arranged in the same order as part two of this book:

SPARKLING WINES AND CHAMPAGNES
These nearly always improve with keeping, even if only for six months, as the extra bottle-age makes the wines richer and more biscuity. If you know a big celebration is coming up, it is well worth buying a year in advance – providing you have tasted the wine and are sure of its quality.

Sparkling wines will stay fizzy for a day easily, sometimes much longer, once opened. To keep the fizz in, if you haven't got a champagne stopper, a teaspoon in the neck of the bottle seems to do the trick, although I am at a loss to explain why!

LIGHT DRY WHITES
Drink within two years of purchase. Once opened drink within 24 hours.

FULL-BODIED DRY WHITES
These will last a lot longer than lighter whites,

especially the better quality ones like burgundy. The best (and most expensive) can last over 20 years. Best drunk within 24 hours once opened.

MEDIUM-DRY AND SPICY WHITES
At the cheaper end, don't keep these more than a year and drink them up fast once opened. However, at the top end of the range (the best Alsace wines, for example) they can last for decades, as well as a day or two once opened.

SWEET WHITES
These are generally fine for up to five years, and the better, more expensive ones can last for decades. Sweet whites will stay fresher for much longer than most wines, once opened, preserved by the extra sugar and alcohol. A week to ten days in the fridge is normally safe.

LIGHT REDS
These tend to be best drunk within a year of purchase, when the fruit is at its juiciest. But tasting experiments with good Beaujolais Nouveau have proved the Gamay grape can still taste good after a few years. Don't keep them for much more than 24 hours after opening.

MEDIUM-BODIED REDS
These will last for three to four years safely, although some can improve over a longer period.

FULL-BODIED REDS
The extra tannin in these wines means they can be kept, and will improve, long term. Anything up to five years is normal, and, in the case of the top wines, ten to 15 years is the minimum.

ROSÉS
These are most enjoyable when drunk young, say within a year of their vintage, as at this time they are at their fruitiest and freshest. The exception to this is rosé champagne, which will improve with some extra bottle-age.

LIQUEURS
The stronger liqueurs and spirits can be kept for ever (well, almost!), and quality is not affected whether the bottle has been opened or not. Remember though, the lower the alcoholic strength, the more susceptible the liqueur is to change, and those like cassis are much better when not kept for too long.

HOW TO USE THE STYLE GUIDE

The wines described in *A Bootful of Wine* are those most commonly seen on French supermarket shelves, the odd exceptions being some of the great names, which I have included here as reference points. This book is not intended to be a comprehensive guide to every French wine.

The style sections

In Part Two of *A Bootful of Wine* the wines have been divided into nine different style categories, plus a small section describing liqueur flavours. The style category sections are as follows:

- Sparkling Wines
- Light Dry Whites
- Full-Bodied Dry Whites
- Medium-Dry and Spicy Whites
- Sweet Whites
- Light Reds
- Medium-Bodied Reds
- Full-Bodied Reds
- Rosés
- Liqueurs and Others

Each section begins with a thumbnail sketch about that particular wine style, how the wines are made, and what foods are best served with them.

Individual wine entries follow, organised alphabetically for easiest possible reference. Because wine producers often make different styles of wine within a given appellation, a certain amount of generalisation has been necessary and I have put wines into the style section they most often adhere to.

For each wine the following information is given.

Pronunciation

Underneath each wine entry there is an easy phonetic spelling of how its name should be pronounced. Using these, you can tell your friends with confidence which wines you have bought. You can even become an overnight wine snob with a decent French accent if you want!

Quality level

There are three quality categories which are indicated by the abbreviations that follow. Quality classifications in France are explained in more detail in Chapter 2, 'Understanding the Label', (*see* pages 20–22).

VDP   Vin de Pays
VDQS   Vin Delimité de Qualité Supérieure
AC   Appellation Contrôlée

Grape varieties

Abbreviations showing the principal grape variety or varieties from which the wine is made are listed too. Where two different varieties are shown, the first one is the more dominant in the blend.

In each style section a key to the abbreviations is repeated every few pages. To see what the grapes taste like, refer to Chapter 4 (pages 29–41), which describes them in detail.

This approach is very useful if you want to try other wines and be safe in the knowledge that you will like them. Just look through the wine entries to find out the grape variety from which your favourite wines are made, and then look up others made from the same grapes.

Price guide

There may be exceptions, but in general these price codes give a fair indication of roughly what you will be paying for your wine. This is designed purely as a guide, though, and is not definitive.

F   Cheap: less than 20 francs a bottle.
FF   Medium: 20 to 70 francs a bottle.
FFF   Expensive: more than 70 francs a bottle.

Wine description

This will give you the details about the wine: where it comes from, what it tastes like, how available it is. Most importantly, it will tell you if it is a good buy for the Bootful or not. In many cases recommended producers are shown too.

– CHAPTER 6 –

SPARKLING WINES

Nothing conjures up an instant celebration like the sound of a popping champagne cork. And it's not only genuine champagne that creates a party atmosphere – all sparkling wine is under pressure, so there will always be a satisfying 'pop' when you open a bottle.

A Bootful of sparkling wine provides you with an even bigger saving than still wine as the duty rates you no longer have to pay are almost double. For each bottle you'll save yourself £1.83, plus the VAT. So although the allowance is less (60 litres compared to 90), it is definitely worthwhile investing in some sparklers.

France has a long history of producing excellent quality sparkling wines of many different styles. And the great thing is that there's one to suit every palate and pocket.

If you have a big celebration coming up, such as a wedding, a christening or a party, now's your chance to show off and treat your guests to bubbly without breaking the bank.

Sparkling wines are the traditional aperitifs, and people will seldom refuse a glass. They are brilliant for parties, and the whole performance of opening the bottles just adds to the sense of occasion. If you want to achieve the racing driver effect of spraying the fizz everywhere, shake the bottle

51

before you open it, but be careful when opening never to point the cork in anyone's direction. If you'd rather keep the maximum fizz in the wine, the trick is to remember to turn the bottle around the cork when opening it. The cork will then pop out with a gentle sigh and none of the precious bubbles will be wasted.

If you prefer a richer, more full-bodied sparkling wine, go for a Blanc de Blancs (white wine made from white grapes), a vintage wine or a rosé. You can serve these with any type of food, providing it is not too highly spiced or strongly flavoured.

While some people frown on it, I especially enjoy a glass of bubbly with pudding as the bubbles seem to cut through sweet flavours. But remember, you can drink a glass of good fizz at any time, so it is essential you leave space for some in your Bootful!

VINS MOUSSEUX

These are the cheapest sparkling wines, many of which are made like lemonade, by carbonation: the fermented grape juice is injected with carbon dioxide. Alternatively, they may undergo their second fermentation in huge sealed tanks. The resulting bubbles are trapped in the wine which is then bottled under pressure.

Because these wines are not generally of *appellation contrôlée* quality, there are fewer restrictions, and the grape juice used to make them can come from anywhere in France. There are many different brands from which to choose too.

If you prefer a dry sparkler, look for the words '*sec*' on the label, and for medium dry, '*demi-sec*'.

Vins mousseux are great inexpensive party wines, ideal for either drinking on their own, or mixed with orange juice to make Bucks Fizz, peach juice to make a Bellini, or a drop of cassis (blackcurrant liqueur) or framboise (raspberry liqueur) for a Kir Royale.

MÉTHODE CHAMPENOISE

According to the Champenoise (the people who live in the Champagne region), this is by far the most sophisticated method of making sparkling wine. They have a certain bias of course, but I tend to agree.

During the *méthode champenoise* process, the still wine undergoes a second fermentation actually inside the bottle and the resulting bubbles are trapped there. Meanwhile, the spent yeast which has transformed the grape sugar into alcohol and carbon dioxide falls to the bottom of the bottle and is then cleverly extracted so that the wine has no sediment when it is eventually opened and poured.

Wines made by this process tend to have much more depth of flavour, and a richer, more biscuity character. Their bubbles also last for much longer in the glass, and all of them have definitely passed their fizzical!

Champagne is the most famous (and most expensive) *méthode champenoise* wine of them all. Genuine champagne can only come from the region in the north of France which bears the same name. It is made from Chardonnay and Pinot Noir grapes, and some Pinot Meunier too.

When buying the 'Grandes Marques' (the well known champagne brands like Moët & Chandon, Lanson, Veuve Clicquot, Mumm, Cordon Rouge, Bollinger, Roederer, etc), make sure you check the prices carefully. Despite the duty saving they can sometimes be found cheaper in Britain. It is also worth experimenting with wines from smaller, less well-known producers.

Many other regions in France have also been making sparkling wines using the champagne method for centuries. Currently these wines carry the words '*méthode champenoise*' on the label and therefore can be easily distinguished from sparkling wines made by other methods. But EC legislation due to come into force in September 1994 will forbid the use of this expression for anything other than champagne. Instead, wines made by this method will carry the words '*méthode traditionnelle*'.

Look out for *méthode champenoise* from the Loire Valley, (Saumur, Vouvray and Crémant de Loire), Burgundy (Crémant de Bourgogne), Alsace (Crémant d'Alsace), and the Rhône Valley (Clairette de Die). These are all serious bubbles for the Bootful.

CRÉMANT
This term simply means the wine is slightly less fizzy than *méthode champenoise*, with a softer, gentler, slightly lighter sparkle.

ROSÉ
Rosé sparkling wines are made by leaving the colour-giving skins from the black grapes in contact with the grape juice until the required colour is reached. This traditional method is, however, notoriously difficult to control, so today the majority of sparkling wine and champagne producers opt for an easier system: still red wine (produced in the same appellation) is simply mixed with the white; a much simpler way of maintaining a consistent colour from year to year.

The Wines

KEY TO GRAPE VARIETY ABBREVIATIONS
Ch   Chardonnay
CB   Chenin Blanc
PN   Pinot Noir
Mxd   Mixed

Blanquette de Limoux   AC   Mxd   FF
(*blon-ket der lee-moo*)

This is produced in the sunny south of France, south of the walled city of Carcassonne, from vineyards which surround the town of Limoux. Here vignerons claim to make France's oldest sparkling wine, said to have first been made by the local monks at St-Hilaire.

It is made from a mixture of grapes including Mauzac, the white leaves of which give the wine its name. Chardonnay and Chenin Blanc are the other two grapes which combine to produce a bubbly with a sherbety character and an attractive dry, yet fruity fizz.

Recommended producers include the largest, most consistent cooperative, Producteurs de Blanquette de Limoux – worth a visit if you are in the area.

Champagne   AC   Ch/PN   FF–FFF
(*sham-pain*)

The best known sparkling wine in the world, there is nothing quite like a glass of good champagne. Produced in one of France's most northerly vineyards, the champagne-makers proudly protect the name of their product, even objecting if the word 'champagne' is used to advertise chocolate bars.

Good champagne is worth the money, although there are tastier (and, more to the point, cheaper) French sparkling wines which are much better buys than inferior champagne.

Non-vintage champagne (a blend of several vintages) is often far greater value than the single vintage variety and tends to be more reliable, reflecting the individual style of the blender rather than the characteristics of a particular year.

The majority of champagnes are made from blends of Chardonnay, Pinot Noir and Pinot Meunier, but each champagne house's wine has its own unique character, and after trying a few you will soon discover which are your favourites. Generally, good champagne has small bubbles and a good *mousse* which keeps on bubbling for a while; also a rich, slightly vanilla-like aroma. If dry, the best champagne will have an attractive, biscuity, lightly toasted flavour and will not be aggressively acidic.

With cheap wines available from smaller producers, try a bottle with your picnic before buying case-loads. Arriving home to discover you have bucket-loads of acidic and undrinkable champagne will leave a nasty taste in your mouth.

Recommended producers include Billecart-Salmon, Bollinger, Charles Heidsieck, Henriot, Jacquart, Jacquesson, Krug, Lanson, Laurent-Perrier, Mercier, Moët & Chandon, Perrier-Jouët, Pol Roger, Louis Roederer, Ruinart and Veuve Clicquot-Ponsardin.

GRAPE VARIETIES FOR SPARKLING WINES		PRICE CODE	
Ch	Chardonnay	F	Cheap: less than 20 francs a bottle.
CB	Chenin Blanc	FF	Medium: 20–70 francs a bottle.
PN	Pinot Noir		
Mxd	Mixed	FFF	Expensive: more than 70 francs a bottle.

Clairette de Die	AC	Mxd	FF
(*clay-ret der dee*)			

This is produced just south of the big blockbuster red territory of the northern Rhône where wines like Hermitage come from. Clairette de Die is an attractive, easy-drinking, floral, spicy sparkler, made from pungent Clairette, and tropical-fruit flavoured Muscat grapes. While sweet on the bouquet, on the palate it is medium dry with a pleasant, lingering, flowery flavour. This is an unusual and worthwhile bubbly for your Bootful.
 Recommended: Cave Coopérative de Die

Crémant d'Alsace	AC	Mxd	FF
(*cray-mon dall-sass*)			

Alsace has changed hands so many times that many people still mistakenly think it is part of Germany. While the architecture and the food are somewhat Germanic, the wines are definitely French in style.
 This bubbly is made from a mixture of grape varieties but still has a touch of the traditional Alsace spiciness in its bouquet and flavour, while being dry on the finish. The rosé is good too, with an earthy, slightly raspberry aroma.
 Recommended producers include Dopff & Irion, Dopff au Moulin, Willy Gisselbrecht, Laugel, and the *caves coopératives*.

Crémant de Bourgogne	AC	Ch/PN	FF
(*cray-mon der bore-goyn-ya*)			

Produced in Burgundy from two of the same grapes as used in the Champagne region (Chardonnay and

Pinot Noir), this is one of France's most attractive sparkling wines. Tasted blind (with its identity kept secret) many people would mistake it for champagne, yet it is sold at roughly half the price! While dry, it has a rich, biscuity aroma, a lightly toasted flavour, and lots of refreshing sparkling fruit on the finish.

As it is a *'crémant'* (*see* the introduction to this chapter, page 53), its sparkle is much softer and less aggressive than that of many sparkling wines.

Also look out for the rosé version of this delicious wine, which has a more marked, almost creamy raspberry flavour. Definitely a good bubbly for the Bootful.

Recommended producers include Caves de Bailly, and Cave Coopérative de Viré.

Crémant de Loire   AC   Mxd   FF
(*cray-mon der l-whar*)

Driving through the stunning Loire Valley with its fairy-tale châteaux where once the kings and queens of France lived, it seems only fitting that this beautiful area should produce quality sparkling wine.

Made predominantly from the earthy, lightly honeyed grape, Chenin Blanc, Crémant de Loire has its own distinctive character: a honeysuckle aroma and dry, slightly appley fruit flavours. Rosé fizz is produced in this appellation too. Those with a sweeter tooth should look for the words *'demi-sec'* on the label.

Recommended producers include Caves de la Loire, Cave Coopérative des Vignerons de Saumur, Gratien & Meyer, Langlois-Château, and also Veuve Amiot.

Saumur	AC	CB	FF
(*so-mure*)			

As with Crémant de Loire, producers have been making sparkling Saumur for centuries. The Champenoise must be impressed, as several important champagne houses own companies and vineyards in this part of the Loire Valley.

Saumur is characterised by an aroma of white-currants and honeysuckle, and lots of easy-drinking sparkling fruit flavour on the palate. The rosé, produced from the Cabernet Franc grape, has a marked red fruit aroma and flavour. *Demi-sec* wines are produced too.

Recommended producers include Aimé-Boucher, Bouvet-Ladubay, Cave Coopérative des Vignerons de Saumur, Gratien & Meyer, Langlois-Château, Rémy Pannier, and Veuve Amiot.

Vouvray	AC	CB	FF
(*voo-vray*)			

Under the vineyards of this Loire region lie miles of underground limestone tunnels and cellars. Not only does this type of rock make excellent storage facilities for sparkling wine, it also imparts a special flavour to it, giving Vouvray its unique taste.

Imagine honeysuckle mixed with a slightly earthy, honeyed aroma and you will have conjured up that of Vouvray. Dry, with appley fizz to the taste, Vouvray is for those who like sparkling wine with distinctive character. Lots of *demi-sec* wines are also made.

Recommended producers include Marc Brédif, Foreau, Huet, and Prince Poniatowski (Aigle d'Or).

– CHAPTER 7 –

LIGHT DRY WHITES

There are lots of bargain Bootful wines amongst the light dry whites. And if you have enjoyed Muscadet over the years you will find a whole host of other similar wines to choose from in this style section. Many of them may have unfamiliar sounding names, but don't worry, these tend to be the best bargains of the lot.

The great thing about light dry whites is that they are easy-drinking, useful all-rounders, ideal to have in the fridge or store cupboard for when unexpected guests drop in.

Many of them are from France's attractive Loire Valley, where the temperature, climate and soils are ideally suited for the production of crisp dry wines. This is also the most famous area for Sauvignon Blanc grapes, which produce Sancerre, Pouilly-Fumé and Touraine Sauvignon.

Indeed many light white wines are made from the grassy, fresh and zippy Sauvignon Blanc; its attractive, gooseberry-like, flinty characteristics make it an appealing option all round. If this is one of your favourites, it can be an interesting exercise to try different wines all made from this grape but from different regions, to see how the flavours vary.

The further south you get, the less advisable it becomes to buy wines from this category. The extra sunshine and heat mean the grapes often get over ripe and suffer from a lack of balancing acidity. There are a few good whites from the south, but these are generally heavier in style.

Most of the wines in this section are not the kind of wines which benefit from being kept. They are at their best when drunk young and fresh, generally in the year following the vintage. Those that are slightly fuller-bodied and will benefit from ageing are indicated in the text.

Light dry white wines make ideal aperitifs, though, and you'll find few people object to a glass, especially when chilled. The lightest, slightly blander wines with good acidity, like Gros Plant from the Loire, make the ideal base for spritzers. Just mix half and half with soda water and serve with ice and a slice of cucumber. Another delicious way to drink them is with a fruit liqueur: just add a drop of the well-known blackcurrant liqueur, cassis, or mûre, the blackberry-flavoured one, or even framboise, made from raspberries, and the wine is transformed into a much sweeter and very tasty kir.

Light dry whites also go well with food. The trick is to balance the weight and flavour of the wine with the meal. For instance, if you serve a zippy light white with chicken in a heavy creamy sauce, the wine will be totally overpowered and will end up tasting thin and insipid.

So for these wines choose foods that are light in style too: salads, pastas, soups and plain roast white meats. Some of the slightly fuller Sauvignon Blanc-based wines like Pouilly-Fumé, Sancerre and Sauvignon de St-Bris have an attractive smokey flavour about them. Try these with smoked foods such as smoked salmon, eel and smoked ham; the combination will enhance the flavours of both.

Seafood is the classic match for light dry whites though. If you have ever eaten a meal in one of the French Atlantic coastal towns you will know what I mean. It is difficult to beat a huge Plateau de Fruits-de-Mer (a cold dish of crabs, mussels, lobsters, whelks, langoustines, clams, cockles, mussels and oysters on a bed of seaweed and crushed ice) accompanied by an ice-cold bottle of Muscadet.

The wines in this section are not only very versatile, but great bargains for your Bootful – particularly if you are adventurous and willing to try some of those which are less well known.

The Wines

KEY TO GRAPE VARIETY ABBREVIATIONS

A	Aligoté
Ch	Chardonnay
CB	Chenin Blanc
GP	Gros Plant
M	Muscadet
PB	Pinot Blanc
SB	Sauvignon Blanc
Sém	Sémillon
Sém/SB	Sémillon/Sauvignon Blanc blend
Mxd	Mixed

Anjou (*on-sjoo*)	AC	CB	F

Although known principally for its production of medium-sweet rosé, this Loire Valley region, stretching to the southwest of Angers and Saumur, produces lots of straightforward, everyday dry drinkable whites.

These are for those who like their wines really

dry, with that mouth-puckering tang of acidity and green appley edge given by the Chenin Blanc grape. Anjou Blanc is ideal for mixing with soda water to make crisp, refreshing spritzers, or with a drop of rich, sweet, blackcurrant-flavoured cassis to make kir.

| **Aude** | VDP | Mxd | F |
| *(ode)* | | | |

The Aude is in the Languedoc-Roussillon region of southern France, with vineyards around Carcassonne and Corbières, sandwiched between the *vin de pays* vineyards of the Hérault and the Pyrénées-Orientales. The whole area produces over 70% of France's *vins de pays*, with Aude the most important *département* of the region. You'll see Aude wines everywhere in France, although reds predominate, making up 90% of production.

Whites are made from a mixture of grapes, mostly the spicy Clairette (the same as for the sparkling wine, *see* page 57) and the blander Grenache Blanc, Ugni Blanc and Macabeo. They are ordinary dry whites which must be drunk young and are definitely for glugging rather than talking about.

| **Beaujolais** | AC | Ch/A | FF |
| *(bow-sjol-ay)* | | | |

Many people are surprised to learn that this region produces white wines as well as the much more famous reds. Accounting for less than 1% of the region's wines, Beaujolais Blanc is occasionally found in some French supermarkets.

A blend of Chardonnay and Aligoté grapes, this is a dry white wine which is easy-drinking, not too acidic, and lightly flowery: great as an aperitif and with fish. It's worth leaving some space in your Bootful for this unusual one.

Bergerac Sec   AC Sém/SB   F
(*bare-sjer-ack seck*)

Perhaps because of the popularity of the TV detective of the same name, this wine has become increasingly fashionable over the last five years or so. The vineyards are found to the east of the city of Bordeaux and the wines are similar in style to light Bordeaux whites.

Sauvignon Blanc grapes give them a crisp, dry fruit flavour, and any rasping acidity is prevented by the softening influence of the Sémillon grape. Quality is fairly consistent.

Recommended producers include Château La Jaubertie, run by Henry Ryman, previously of the famous stationery chain of the same name.

Bordeaux   AC Sém/SB   F
(*bore-doe*)

Bordeaux is famous for its wonderful red and sweet white wines, so all too often its dry whites get overlooked. The good news for the consumer is that, as a result, they can be great value for money.

Light white Bordeaux wines can come from anywhere in the huge Gironde region, and, until recent years were often tired, old-style and very boring. But many producers have cleaned up their act and, using modern vinification techniques, are now making delicious, fresh and exciting wines. The best are quality dry whites with more substance and body than many – ideal for the Bootful.

Bouches du Rhône	VDP	Mxd	F

(*boosh dew rone*)

Produced in the south of France, these wines come from a large area which encompasses Provence and the Camargue. As in most areas in the south, the red wines are more common, but the quality of the whites is improving daily.

Grapes used include the bland Ugni Blanc which is blended with the more spicy Clairette and flowery Muscat. Increasingly, producers are planting Chardonnay to give the wines more depth and, as this grape is so popular, some producers' wines now name it on the label.

Bouches du Rhône are mid-weight, with some spicy underlying fruit, sometimes suffering from the opposite problem to many dry whites in that they can lack that certain bite of acidity. Generally good value for money and worth including in your Bootful.

Bourgogne	AC	Ch	F–FF

(*bore-goyn-ya*)

Wines sold with this appellation can come from anywhere within the Burgundy region.

Made from the Chardonnay grape, they can

GRAPE VARIETIES FOR LIGHT DRY WHITE WINES		
A	Aligoté	
Ch	Chardonnay	
CB	Chenin Blanc	
GP	Gros Plant	
M	Muscadet	
PB	Pinot Blanc	
SB	Sauvignon Blanc	
Sém	Sémillon	

Sém/SB	Sémillon/ Sauvignon Blanc blend
Mxd	Mixed

PRICE CODE

F	Cheap: less than 20 francs a bottle.
FF	Medium: 20–70 francs a bottle.
FFF	Expensive: more than 70 francs a bottle.

range from light, easy-drinking dry whites to slightly richer, more biscuity wines from the better producers. When you find one you like, make sure you make a note of the producer's name as quality varies so much. At their best, they are whitecurrant-flavoured dry whites with a biscuity, buttery edge, and can be delicious when served with food.

Recommended producers include Bouzereau, Drouhin, Jadot, Jaffelin, Labouré-Roi, Lamblin, Latour, Leflaive, Mommessin and Remoissenet.

Bourgogne Aligoté AC A FF
(*bore-goyn-ya al-ee-goat-ay*)

This is for those who enjoy really bone dry wines with a zippy, acidic kick, and will come as an unpalatable shock to those not used to them! It is often drunk in the region mixed with the blackcurrant liqueur, cassis, to make kir. Generally on the thin side, this is an aperitif rather than a food wine.

Corbières (*kor-bee-air*) AC Mxd F

Like many areas in the sunny south of France, this region is better known for its red wines. The white is made from a blend of local grapes including Clairette, Grenache and Muscat, and is light and clean, with faintly spicy undertones. Easy drinking, uncomplicated, good as an aperitif, and a sure bet for the Bootful.

Coteaux de l'Ardèche VDP Ch/SB F
(*cot-oh der lard-esh*)

This important *vin de pays* area lies to the west of the Rhône Valley. As well as local varieties, growers are increasingly using Chardonnay and Sauvignon Blanc for the whites, grapes that will be named on the labels. Chardonnays tend to be the light white-currant style, and Sauvignons, dry without being too grassy or acidic. Definitely a good value area to watch; this is certainly a wine for the Bootful.

Coteaux du Lyonnais AC Ch/A F
(*cot-oh dew lee-on-aise*)

Sandwiched between Beaujolais vineyards to the north, and the Côtes du Rhône vineyards to the south, this is a relatively small, unfashionable area whose wines are worth looking out for. They are made from Chardonnay and Aligoté and tend to be of light to medium weight, dry with good depth of fruit. Good with food and normally much better value than Bourgogne Aligoté.

Côtes de Blaye AC Sém/SB F
(*coat der bly*)

Blaye lies on the opposite side of the river Gironde to Bordeaux's famous red wine producing area, the Médoc. While little known in Britain, this region has a long history of winemaking dating back to Roman times.

Britain's wine buyers have only recently caught on, and this is definitely an up-and-coming region to watch for both red and white wines as the quality and affordable prices make a great combination. Originally, most of the white wine produced here was thin, tart and acidic, and much was distilled to make cognac. But happily, some interesting and very drinkable wines are now to be seen.

Côtes de Blayes are characterised by zippy, upfront fruit, with lots of fresh, gooseberrry-like Sauvignon character. Those wines with an added dash of spice probably contain a percentage of Muscadelle grapes. Increasingly these are a good buy for the Bootful.

Côtes de Gascogne	VDP	Mxd	F
(*coat der gas-coyn*)			

No, not named after the famous footballer, but he almost certainly helps people to pronounce the name of this now fashionable dry white *vin de pays*. Not surprisingly, it crops up more often in British supermarkets than it does in France.

This is made in Three Musketeer country, a region more famous for its production of armagnac than wine. Grapes used include Colombard, Ugni Blanc and Gros Manseng, and produce a zippy, tangy, refreshing white, with good fruit and acidity. The quality is fairly consistent. A sound choice for the Bootful.

Recommended producers include Domaine Grassa, which has had so much success in recent years in Britain.

Côtes de Thau	VDP	Mxd	F
(*coat der toe*)			

Vineyards in this region flourish along the edge of the Mediterranean coast, to the southwest of the port of Sète in the Hérault district of the huge Languedoc-Roussillon region. Don't worry if this is an unfamiliar name – until recently most Côtes de Thau grapes were used to make vermouth, not wine. Now its *vin de pays* status has changed all that and many more Bootful bargains are to be found.

The whites are light and dry with a slight spiciness, derived from blending the Clairette grape with Ugni Blanc and Terret Blanc. These are easy-drinking everyday wines, ideal for large parties.

| **Côtes du Rhône** | AC | Mxd | F |
| *(coat dew rone)* | | | |

More commonly seen in France than in England, white Côtes du Rhône is nothing like as well known as its red blooded brother (*see* pages 141–42). Until a few years ago the whites tended to lack acidity and were bland and boring, but new winemaking techniques have begun to change the situation and now some tasty bargain whites are emerging.

The same blend of grapes is permitted for the whites as the reds, the colour-giving skins of the red grapes being removed quickly after pressing so that they don't colour the wines.

Côtes du Rhône Blancs have more weight than many dry whites, with a distinctly sun-baked grapey aroma and a refreshing tang of acidity on the finish. Far less bland, they are also something of an acquired taste, so do try a few bottles first before adding them to your Bootful.

| **Entre-Deux-Mers** | AC | Sém/SB | F |
| *(on-trer der mare)* | | | |

'Between two seas' is the direct translation of the name of this wine region, so called because of its position between two of Bordeaux's most famous rivers, the Dordogne and the Garonne. The largest district in Bordeaux, lots of fantastic-value white wines are now produced here thanks to new methods of winemaking where refrigeration makes the wines much cleaner and fresher tasting.

Mainly made from a blend of the crisp, grassy Sauvignon Blanc and the softer, richer Sémillon grape, some wines also have a little Muscadelle in their blend which gives them a delicate, lightly perfumed aroma and flavour. Good value wines, the best of which are well suited for drinking on special occasions. Keep a place for them in your Bootful!

Recommended producers include Châteaux Bonnet, Moulin-de-Launay, Peyrabon and Thieuley.

| **Gers** (*jair*) | VDP | Mxd | F |

Not often seen in Britain, this wine is well-known in France. It comes from the Midi-Pyrenees region to the southeast of Bordeaux, around the city of Auch. While it has a less fashionable name, the white is similar in style to Vin de Pays de Gascogne (*see* page 68).

Fresh, easy-drinking, with a refreshing fruity tang, Gers wines are cheap enough to enjoy at any time, especially when bought by the Bootful.

| **Gros Plant** (*grow plon*) | VDQS | GP | F |

Gros Plant is like a lesser Muscadet, produced in the same part of the Loire Valley but even drier in style. It is made from the Gros Plant grape – rather than the Muscadet – which is characterised by a rasping acidity and bone dry, zippy flavour. If you normally like medium-dry wines this one could present you with a very unpleasant shock.

As it is not an *appellation contrôlée* wine it is much cheaper than Muscadet and, provided you like its incredible dryness, it is a good buy. You can always soften it up by adding a drop of cassis to make a much sweeter, refreshing kir.

Recommended producers include Donatien-Bahuaud, Chéreau-Carré, Guilbaud, and Sauvion.

Haut-Poitou   VDQS Mxd   FF
(*oh pwa-too*)

Haut-Poitou wines are great value, and their quality excellent. Situated in the Loire Valley, southwest of Tours, the best producer in this region is the large cooperative. They make both Sauvignon and Chardonnay based wines; the former the most successful, with an attractive crisp, green grassy aroma, and flinty dry flavour: it's rather like a mini Sancerre, but much cheaper. The Chardonnay is of the light, zippy kind and makes a good aperitif. Definitely a name to look out for, its quality improving every day.

Recommended producers include the excellent *cave coopérative*.

Jurançon Sec   AC Mxd   FF
(*sjure-on-sonn-seck*)

This comes from vineyards situated in the foothills of the Pyrenees, where the Romans first planted vines. Jurançon is a peculiar wine and one which

GRAPE VARIETIES FOR LIGHT DRY WHITE WINES		Sém/SB	Sémillon/ Sauvignon Blanc blend
A	Aligoté	Mxd	Mixed
Ch	Chardonnay	**PRICE CODE**	
CB	Chenin Blanc	F	Cheap: less than 20 francs a bottle.
GP	Gros Plant		
M	Muscadet	FF	Medium: 20–70 francs a bottle.
PB	Pinot Blanc		
SB	Sauvignon Blanc	FFF	Expensive: more than 70 francs a bottle.
Sém	Sémillon		

does not easily fit into any one category; wines labelled simply 'Jurançon' are much sweeter than Jurançon Sec, and tend to have even more spicy fruitiness (*see* page 96).

Made from a blend of grapes, including Gros Manseng, Petit Manseng and Corbu, even this, the dry wine, has a touch of spicy sweetness about it, especially on the aroma. Flavours on the palate include pineapple and cinnamon. It is an excellent food wine, and goes especially well with full-bodied, rich dishes such as oily fish and spicy red meat. Make sure you try a bottle before filling your Bootful as it is something of an acquired taste.

Recommended producers include the Cave Coopérative de Jurançon.

Mâcon	AC	Ch	FF
(*mack-on*)			

One of the best-known French dry whites, made from the Chardonnay grape. Dry, light and easy to drink, the better wines exhibit a mixture of white-currant-like fruit, with a fresh touch of butteriness in the taste.

Wines with the appellation Mâcon-Villages tend to be slightly more weighty: richer, and more buttery still, especially those that name the specific village they are from. Mâcon-Chardonnay actually comes from the village after which the fashionable grape variety is named, with the cooperative there producing some really good quality wines. Other villages mentioned on the label and worth looking out for include Clessé, Fuissé, Lugny, Prissé, Vinzelles and Viré.

Recommended producers include the various *caves coopératives* (named after their villages) as well as Boulay, Burrier, Duboeuf, Latour, Loron, Mommessin, Rousset and Thevenet.

Menetou-Salon   AC   SB   FF
(*men-e-too sal-on*)

An uncommon name, but worth remembering as this region produces some of the most interesting wines of the Loire Valley's 'Central Vineyards'. It is situated not far from the better known Sancerre and Pouilly-Fumé appellations.

Made from the Sauvignon Blanc grape, Menetou-Salon wines have an added dimension of fruit, with an almost chocolate-like flavour backing up the gooseberry dry character of the grape.

These are good food wines as they can stand up to fairly highly flavoured food. They are also delicious as alternative aperitifs. Much better value than neighbouring Sancerre as the name is less well known, so fill up your boot!

Recommended producers include Chatenoy, Chavignol, Couer and Mellot.

Mont Bouquet   VDP   Mxd   F
(*mon-boo-kay*)

A *vin de pays* from the productive Languedoc-Roussillon area in the south of France, situated just north of Nîmes.

While over 60% of the wine produced here is red, the whites are worth looking out for too. Made from a blend of Ugni Blanc, Clairette and Grenache Blanc grapes, they are light, easy to drink wines, great as aperitifs or for parties. And as they are little known they tend also to be very good value.

Montagny	AC	Ch	FF
(*mon-tan-yee*)			

A lesser known white burgundy and one which, as a result, can often be a bargain for your Bootful. The village of Montagny is in the south of the Côte Chalonnaise, before you reach the Mâconnais, and its wines represent much better value than those from the latter. Montagny wines vary from light, easy-drinking whites to those with more depth and characteristic buttery richness from the Chardonnay grape.

Recommended producers include Arnoux and the *cave coopérative* at Buxy.

Muscadet	AC	M	F–FF
(*musk-a-day*)			

Travel through the breathtakingly beautiful Loire Valley from the Atlantic Ocean, and the first wine region you will come to is the Pays Nantais, the home of Muscadet. The French developed a taste for this wine during the 1950s when fashionable Paris restaurants could not get enough dry white burgundy and began looking for alternatives.

Made from the grape of the same name (also known as the Melon de Bourgogne), Muscadet is a bone dry wine, with crisp, refreshing acidity. It is the ideal accompaniment for the wonderful and abundant seafood for which the Atlantic coast is famous.

The best quality Muscadet is produced in the Sèvre-et-Maine region, so look out for these words appearing as part of the wine name. If Muscadet is to your taste, you can also look for wines with the words '*sur lie*' on the label (*see* page 24). These are slightly richer, with a yeasty character, and often have a slight spritz, which makes them even more refreshing – expect to pay a little more though.

Recommended producers include Donatien-Bahuaud, Chéreau-Carré, Guilbaud, Louis Métaireau and Sauvion.

Petit Chablis	AC	Ch	FF
(*pet-ee shab-lee*)			

The name means, literally, 'little Chablis'. It is made by the same producers that make Chablis itself – possibly the best known of all white burgundies – and in the same area, right in the north of the region. Petit Chablis vineyards, however, are not as well-situated as those entitled to the full Chablis appellation.

Don't be put off though. A good Petit Chablis can be better than many a Chablis, and it will always be cheaper. Quite possibly a Bootful wine.

Recommended growers: La Chablisienne, Drouhin, Labouré-Roi, Domaine Laroche and Albert Pic.

Pinot Blanc d'Alsace	AC	PB	F–FF
(*pee-no blonk dall-sass*)			

The least aromatic of the Alsace grape varieties, Pinot Blanc nonetheless makes some very attractive wines. They tend to exhibit more fruitiness than spiciness and have a clean flavour with a hint of dry floweriness. Because they are not expensive they can be good Bootful material. (If you like this sort of wine, but want a bit more spiciness, look up other Alsace wines in the Medium-Dry and Spicy Whites chapter, pages 92–99).

Recommended producers include Becker, Beyer,

Blanck, Cattin, Dopff & Irion, Dopff au Moulin, Maison Louis Gisselbrecht, Willy Gisselbrecht, Hugel, Marc Kreydenweiss, Preiss-Zimmer, Rolly Gassmann, Schlumberger, Trimbach and Zind-Humbrecht.

Pouilly-Fumé   AC   SB   FF
(*poo-ee foo-may*)

One of the best known dry whites produced in the Loire Valley, and one which restaurateurs always make us pay through the nose for because they're well aware that people recognise the name.

However, unlike some well-known, expensive wines, Pouilly-Fumé at its best is certainly of very high quality indeed. It is made from the Sauvignon Blanc grape, and is characterised by crisp, gooseberry fruit and an unusual, slightly smokey, flinty aftertaste, hence the its name 'Fumé', meaning smoked. Perhaps its only word suggestion, but a glass or two of Pouilly certainly goes down very well with smoked food.

By the way, don't mistake Pouilly-Fumé for Pouilly-Fuissé: the latter is quite different – it is a burgundy made from the Chardonnay grape (*see* pages 89–90).

Recommended producers: Bailly, Dagueneau, Dezat, Ladoucette, Laporte, Redde, Saget and Château de Tracy.

Pouilly Vinzelles   AC   Ch   FF
(*poo-ee van-zell*)

Produced in the Mâconnais region of Burgundy, next door to Pouilly-Fuissé (*see* pages 89–90), the wines of this appellation tend to be lighter, with easy-drinking fresh Chardonnay fruit. Being less well known, they can be good value, though they rarely achieve the same richness as their more prestigious neighbours. Similar in style to good Mâcon.

Recommended producers include Burrier, Duboeuf, Loron and Mommessin and Vincent.

Quincy (*can-see*)   AC   SB   FF

Like Bergerac, Quincy also shares the same name as a television detective. It's worth doing a spot of detective work to search it out. It comes from next door to the much more famous Sancerre appellation (*see* page 78), and is therefore of a similar style; being less renowned, however, it is much better value for money. Good Bootful material!

Don't try to pronounce Quincy in the same way as you would the television detective's name though, you'll be met by lots of blank faces. Instead, try saying 'can-see' and hopefully you'll be led to a shelf where indeed you can see some bottles!

Crisp and dry, Quincy combines a green grassy aroma with tangy, refreshing, gooseberry flavours. It is a great aperitif, and is delicious with seafood and fish.

GRAPE VARIETIES FOR LIGHT DRY WHITE WINES		Sém/SB	Sémillon/ Sauvignon Blanc blend
A	Aligoté	Mxd	Mixed
Ch	Chardonnay	**PRICE CODE**	
CB	Chenin Blanc	F	Cheap: less than 20 francs a bottle.
GP	Gros Plant		
M	Muscadet	FF	Medium: 20–70 francs a bottle.
PB	Pinot Blanc		
SB	Sauvignon Blanc	FFF	Expensive: more than 70 francs a bottle.
Sém	Sémillon		

Recommended growers include Berri, Besombes, Houssier, Mardon, Mellot, Pipet and Rapin.

Rully (*roo-ee*)	AC	Ch	FF

A high quality, but little known white from the north of Burgundy's Côte Chalonnaise region. Good Rully is a very good buy. It is made from Burgundy's classic Chardonnay grape and so has the delicious buttery flavours found in the famous Côte d'Or wines. Nevertheless, because it tends not to be aged in oak, it is a bit lighter than its northern brothers and can be drunk younger. The best Rullys are fresh, crisp, light, tasty and easy to drink.

Don't confuse Rully with Reuilly, which is also good value but from near Quincy and Menetou-Salon in the Loire and made from the Sauvignon Blanc grape.

Recommended producers include Duvernay, Jacqueson and Château de Rully.

Sancerre (*son-sare*)	AC	SB	FF

This pretty hilltop village in the Central Vineyard region of the Loire Valley produces one of France's most famous dry white wines, enjoyed in restaurants throughout the world. Sancerre at its best is delicious, with attractive green, grassy aromas and crisp, refreshing acidity, fully justifying the hype. However, because of the price it commands, many mediocre producers have jumped on the bandwagon and are producing Sancerre that is little better than cheap table wine.

Because of this, unless you can find a really good Sancerre producer whose style you enjoy, it is often worth buying the much cheaper wines from neighbouring appellations like Menetou-Salon, Quincy and Reuilly.

Although Sancerre is now famous for its white wines, it is interesting to note that, until the late 19th century, it was predominantly a red wine producing region.

Recommended producers include Archambault, Bailly, Bourgeois, Delaporte, Dezat, Laporte, Mellot, Prieur, Vacheron and Vatan. There are many others and it is always worth experimenting with a bottle before buying a Bootful.

Saumur (*so-mure*)	AC	CB	F–FF

Crisp, dry, inexpensive whites are made in this attractive region of the Loire Valley. The Chenin Blanc grape producing wines with dry, yet slightly honeyed fruit, a flowery aroma, and underlying earthiness. Occasionally growers add up to 20% Chardonnay or Sauvignon Blanc to give their wines a bit of extra body.

Saumur's distinctive flavours make it the ideal foil for the many river fish dishes served in restaurants in the Loire Valley. If you enjoy Saumur sparkling wine which is made from the same grape (*see* page 59), you'll enjoy these very drinkable still whites too.

Sauvignon de St-Bris	VDQS	SB	F–FF
(*so-veen-yon der san-bree*)			

A bit of an oddity from northern Burgundy, and as a result, great value for money. While neighbouring Chablis grows Chardonnay exclusively, this little village sticks its neck out and produces classy Sauvignon Blanc wines, even though this grape is, in

Burgundy, not entitled to *appellation contrôlée* status.

The wine is generally not aged in oak barrels, and so is crisp and dry, with a classic fresh grassy aroma. The best has wonderful gooseberry-like fruit on the palate, with a deliciously smokey aftertaste, making it ideal with any type of smoked or barbecued food. These whites are designed for early drinking rather than keeping. A classy bargain, well worth including in a Bootful!

Recommended producers include Brocard, Lamblin and Sorin.

Touraine (*too-rain*)   AC   SB   F

Easy-drinking dry whites are produced in this region of the Loire Valley, from vineyards surrounding the ancient city of Tours. The range of wines produced under the Touraine appellation is very large, covering both sweet and dry whites, rosés and reds.

Unlike neighbouring Saumur, Touraine whites are made from the Sauvignon Blanc grape, whose nettle-like, green grassy, gooseberry flavoured characteristics have made Sancerre the popular wine it is today. The best Touraine Sauvignons are as good as Sancerre, but a lot cheaper, so essential Bootful material. Always look for the youngest vintage available as the beauty of these wines is shown in their youth when they are more fragrant, crisp and thirst-quenching.

Producers are numerous and it's best to experiment yourself to see which ones you prefer.

– CHAPTER 8 –

FULL-BODIED DRY WHITES

If you've ever enjoyed a decent Chablis or Meursault, the chances are that you enjoy reasonably full-bodied white wines. These are wines that are for savouring and enjoying rather than just gulping down. They have many layers of different flavours and are at their best with food.

The majority of wines in this category are made from Chardonnay, an extremely versatile grape. It can produce quite light, zippy whites like Mâcon, or, with a bit of help from some oak barrels for maturation, as well as the best possible vineyard location, it can produce gloriously rich, buttery wines with lots of dry fruit and a touch of vanilla on the finish. There are a whole host of Chardonnay styles that fall in between these categories, but it is the full-bodied blockbusters that appear here.

Chardonnay shows off its best colours in Burgundy, the region which produces some of the world's classic dry whites like Meursault and Le Montrachet. These wines, when made by good producers, are mind-blowing, unequalled anywhere else in the world.

Unfortunately, for those of us looking for a bargain Bootful, Burgundy is not really the best area to explore. Because of a limited supply, prices for the best known white burgundies, although coming down, will never be cheap.

Nevertheless, as you'll see from the entries in this section, all is not lost for the persistent bargain seeker. If you are prepared to experiment with a few relatively unknown names you won't be disappointed, as, by selecting carefully, there are some great buys to be had: St-Romain, St-Véran, Pernand-Vergelesses and Pouilly-Fuissé to name a few. And then, for the really adventurous, there are the oddballs like Arbois Jaune, produced near the Swiss border.

Although these wines are rarely very cheap ('F' – *see* page 50 for price codes), once tasted, if their style is to your liking, you will probably find you are prepared to venture into the 'FF' price range, and even splash out and buy a few 'FFF' wines for special occasions.

While all the wines in this section can be enjoyed on their own, many people believe such intensity of flavour is best shown off when drunk with a meal.

Richer, more full-bodied wines need to be matched with food of a similar weight. Serve them with a light soufflé or a delicate consommé and the flavour of the wine will swamp the dish. Serve them with a really over-the-top lobster thermidor and the combination will be stunning.

Wines towards the lighter end of the spectrum in this category (Chablis is a good example), can be drunk with more delicately flavoured foods. Fresh-water fish and Chablis are a sensational combination, as is Chablis with roast chicken.

The full-bodied flavour of oak-aged Chardonnay on the other hand, calls for richer dishes and is a good alternative to red wine for drinking with lots of roast meats. The oaky, vanilla flavour of the wine means it will cope admirably with chicken and turkey, not to mention chargrilled or roast red meat dishes like lamb or beef.

The fat butteriness often found in full-bodied white wines makes them the ideal complement for fish dishes, especially those with creamy sauces: salmon and hollandaise, sole meunière or kedgeree. Garlic and spicy Provençale dishes are also a good match.

For anyone who does not like red wines (and also for those of us who do!), these heavy dry whites are an excellent alternative to drink with fully-flavoured food.

The Wines

KEY TO GRAPE VARIETY ABBREVIATIONS
    Ch   Chardonnay
    Sém/SB Sémillon/Sauvignon Blanc blend
    Mxd   Mixed

| **Arbois Jaune** | AC | Mxd | FF |
| *(ahr-bwa sjone)* | | | |

This wine is an oddball, worth searching out if it is to your taste as there is nothing quite like it. Produced from grapes grown in the Jura vineyards near the French border with Switzerland, Vin Jaune is made from a local grape called the Savagnin (not to be confused with Sauvignon). It is aged in oak barrels for around six years, after which, because it has been in contact with oxygen, the wine has turned a deep yellow colour, hence the term '*jaune*', the French word for yellow.

The taste is somewhere between that of a dry sherry and an old madeira, and the longer you keep a bottle the richer and more nutty it becomes. You'll either love it or hate it, so make sure you try some before filling your Bootful!

Auxey-Duresses   AC   Ch   FF–FFF
(*oak-see dure-ess*)

This is one of Burgundy's best kept secrets. The vineyards of Auxey-Duresses are right next door to the famous village of Meursault and produce wines of a very similar style (*see* page 88). However, because the name is not nearly as famous as that of its neighbour, the prices are much lower, and the wines better value. Perhaps its lack of fame is because the name looks difficult to pronounce – it isn't though, *see above*.

Rich and slightly honeyed, Auxey-Duresses has dry, yet complex fruit and needs to be savoured with a meal to realise its full potential.

Don't just go for the big village names when buying burgundy. It's well worth experimenting with a wine like this – reap the rewards of being adventurous. Auxey-Duresses is a great Bootful wine, but make sure you taste a bottle of what you intend to buy before stocking up your car boot as its quality does tend to vary.

Recommended producers include Ampeau, Jaffelin and Leflaive.

Chablis   AC   Ch   FF–FFF
(*shab-lee*)

Probably the world's best known and most often asked for dry white wine.

The name Chablis has been much abused, both by unscrupulous growers in the area and by New

World winemakers looking to associate their wines with this French classic. Certain producers in both continents were aware of the pull of the word 'Chablis', and took advantage of it. Until recently, quality has suffered drastically because of this, and prices have been completely distorted. However, over the last year or two, most French producers seem to have made a real effort to improve quality and control costs, and these wines can once more be well worth the buy.

Although classed as a burgundy, Chablis' vineyards are actually closer to Champagne than they are to the Côte d'Or; making this one of France's most northerly vineyard regions. Chablis creators claim the secret of their wine's distinctive character lies in the particular type of clay soil in which the vines are grown.

Chablis is produced in two very different styles. One is aged in oak and is rich and buttery with a distinct flavour of vanilla. The other is made in stainless steel vats and the result is a much leaner wine with austere crisp, dry fruit. Unfortunately, labels do not say which style the wine is, so you have to take pot luck!

There are four qualities of Chablis: Grand Cru, Premier Cru, Chablis, and Petit Chablis.

Chablis Grand Cru is theoretically the best, and is quite expensive. Premier Cru from a good producer is also significantly better than a straight Chablis; it

GRAPE VARIETIES FOR FULL-BODIED DRY WHITES		PRICE CODE	
Ch	Chardonnay	F	Cheap: less than 20 francs a bottle.
Sém/SB	Sémillon/Sauvignon Blanc blend	FF	Medium: 20–70 francs a bottle.
Mxd	Mixed	FFF	Expensive: more than 70 francs a bottle.

too can be worth the extra. The latter, however, from a good producer, can be a delicious wine. And Petit Chablis, the lightest of them all, comes from the lesser vineyards, but can be excellent Bootful material if chosen carefully.

Recommended producers include La Chablisienne, Drouhin, Labouré-Roi, Domaine Laroche and Albert Pic.

Chassagne-Montrachet   AC   Ch   FFF
(*shass-ann mon-rash-ay*)

One of the greatest white burgundies of the Côte de Beaune. It is never cheap, and so is generally not a wine for your Bootful. However, at its best it is stunning, rich with lots of buttery fruit and long lingering complex flavours on the aftertaste.

This is the kind of great French Chardonnay that producers all over the world try to emulate, rarely with total success. It is a wine worth trying for a special occasion, and will be especially enjoyable, indeed at its best with food. But, if you can, do taste before buying any in quantity: there are good and poor producers in Chassagne-Montrachet, and sampling a few bottles to see whose you prefer will not be a hardship!

As with most Burgundy villages, there are Premier Cru and Grand Cru wines from Chassagne. The latter are not worth buying in supermarkets because their sky-high price ensures they will have been sitting on the shelf for a very long time. The Premier Crus can be worthwhile investments, but are often overpriced.

Recommended producers include Bachelet, Deléger, Gagnard-Delagrange, Lamy, Morey, Ramonet and Roux.

Corton-Charlemagne	AC	Ch	FFF

(*kor-tonn sharler-man-yer*)

Corton-Charlemagne is named after a king, and it probably helps to be one to afford this stunning white burgundy, one the Côte de Beaune's very best wines.

Legend has it that in King Charlemagne's reign the hill of Corton produced only red wines. He loved the wine, but his wife didn't. She got so fed up with the red wine staining his famous white beard that a part of the hill, now this famous vineyard, was replanted with white grapes.

Whatever the truth, Corton-Charlemagne is certainly legendary. Produced in the very north of the region, only a very small amount of this rich, buttery, silky wine is made, hence its heady price. If only we could all afford to load the Bootful with it!

Corton-Charlemagne is one of the very few burgundies for which the quality is likely to be good regardless of the producer.

Graves (*grahv*)	AC	Sém/SB	FF–FFF

This can be one of the world's greatest white wines, and yet it has never caught on with wine-drinkers as a whole. They don't know what they are missing.

White Graves today is a very exciting wine, and the best totally different to the dreary, boring rubbish that used to be sold under this name. It can compete with the best white burgundies but sadly is not Bootful material because of its price.

Recommended producers at the 'FF' level include Châteaux Couhins-Lurton, Smith-Haut-Lafitte and La Louvière, all produced in the Pessac-Léognan appellation (*see* page 154).

Meursault	AC	Ch	FFF
(*mer-so*)			

Almost as well known as Chablis, Meursault is in such demand all over the world that it sells for some extremely high prices. It is one of the most famous wines of Burgundy's Côte de Beaune, and at its best you can expect from it weighty buttery fruit, with ripe nutty vanilla flavours on the palate, and fine balancing acidity. It is a wine best drunk with food.

While all great white burgundies will get better with age (and Meursault is no exception) one of their attractions is that they can be enjoyed when young too.

Premier Cru Meursault is the best available, and the most expensive, and you will often see it with a vineyard name attached: one of the best known is 'Les Charmes'.

Recommended producers include Ampeau, Bouzereau, Coche-Dury, Jean Germain, Jobard, Labouré-Roi, Lafon, Latour, Magenta, Matrot and Morey.

Pernand-Vergelesses	AC	Ch	FF–FFF
(*pear-non vair-jeh-less*)			

This is one of the least well known white burgundies of the Côte de Beaune. Because of this, Pernand-Vergelesses can be great value, and a good Bootful candidate.

The vineyards are in the village of Aloxe-Corton, on adjoining slopes to the great Corton-Charlemagne (*see* page 87). The wines are less rich than the Côte de Beaune's more famous whites, but still have good structure, attractive dry fruit, acidity and lots of lightly buttery flavour on the finish.

The better and more expensive Pernand-Vergelesses have the words Premier Cru on their labels and tend to be more hefty on the palate. Quality, though, can be variable, so if you are investing in any quantity, make sure you have tasted the particular wine you are buying before committing yourself.

Recommended producers include Dubreuil-Fontaine, Laleure-Piot, Leflaive, Rapet and Voarick.

Pouilly-Fuissé   AC   Ch   FF–FFF
(*poo-ee fwee-say*)

Not to be mistaken for the similar sounding Pouilly-Fumé (a Sauvignon Blanc-based wine from the Loire Valley – *see* page 76), this wine is produced in the Mâconnais region of Burgundy. The vineyards lie to the west of the town of Mâcon, just north of St-Véran.

The wines of the Mâconnais are generally much lighter than those of the Côte d'Or further north. However, Pouilly-Fuissé is sometimes an exception and the best can have a surprisingly good dash of Chardonnay butteriness as well as underlying dryness and youthful fruit. Those wines which have been aged in oak barrels have a richer, slightly nutty, vanilla aroma and flavour. The best ones can age well, so it is worth laying some down if – and

GRAPE VARIETIES FOR FULL-BODIED DRY WHITES		PRICE CODE	
Ch	Chardonnay	F	Cheap: less than 20 francs a bottle.
Sém/SB	Sémillon/Sauvignon Blanc blend	FF	Medium: 20–70 francs a bottle.
Mxd	Mixed	FFF	Expensive: more than 70 francs a bottle.

that's a big 'if' – you can find a good one at a reasonable price.

Recommended producers include Besson, Loron, Pacquet and Vincent.

Puligny-Montrachet AC Ch FFF
(*poo-leen-yee mon-rash-ay*)

One of Burgundy's greatest Côte de Beaune whites, Puligny-Montrachet will never be cheap and so regrettably is not really a Bootful wine.

It is finer than its neighbour and rival, Chassagne-Montrachet, and shows the Chardonnay grape at its very best, with masses of butterscotch-like fruit, blended with vanilla, and balanced with steely acidity. The legendary 'Le Montrachet', is a Grand Cru appellation within the Puligny commune, and its wine is even richer and more complex. You would have to be very wealthy to afford just one bottle, and most people would need a mortgage to buy a Bootful.

Recommended producers include Ampeau, Bouzereau, Carillon, Clerc, Leflaive and Sauzet.

St-Romain AC Ch F–FF
(*san row-man*)

One of the best value white wines from Burgundy's Côte d'Or, St-Romain can be superb value. The best are rich and buttery, with great depth of flavour. They are not as well-known as other white burgundies – Chassagne-Montrachet, for example – and so are much cheaper. Sadly, only the more adventurous shops are likely to stock these delicious wines.

Recommended producers include Gras and Thévenin-Monthelie.

| **St-Véran** | AC | Ch | FF |
| *(san vair-on)* | | | |

If you know you like white burgundy but are not so sold on the price, St-Véran is possibly the wine for you. Still relatively unknown, it is produced in the south of the Mâconnais region, which runs south into Beaujolais. Made from the standard white burgundy grape, Chardonnay, this wine combines a light buttery richness with zippy whitecurrant flavour, both characteristic traits of the grape.

Find one you like and invest in it as it's a good all rounder, unusual enough for special occasions yet not too expensive. It is ideal both as an aperitif and as a food wine. Provided your budget will stand it, St-Veran can be great for the Bootful.

Recommended producers include Duboeuf, Luquet and Vincent (very expensive).

| **Savoie** | AC | Mxd | FF |
| *(sav-wahr)* | | | |

You may have tasted this wine without realising it if you are a keen skier, as Savoie's vineyards nestle on the slopes between Lake Geneva and Grenoble.

Made primarily from a mixture of local grape varieties, like Chasselas and Roussette, others such as Chardonnay and Aligoté are also blended in to this wine, to create unusual whites which are dry yet have complexity and a slightly nutty edge.

Definitely an acquired taste, they seem very different without the buzz, *joie de vive* and altitude of the ski-slopes. Experiment by tasting a bottle (preferably at home) before you load up your Bootful.

CHAPTER 9

MEDIUM-DRY AND SPICY WHITES

These wines are some of the most characterful and distinctive of those which deserve a place in your Bootful. Spicy wines have an extraordinary aroma which is like the smell of a spice cabinet, a mixture of cinnamon, ginger and nutmeg. This spiciness is carried through onto the palate too, where you can also often taste the flavours of tropical fruits.

If there are wines in this section that you are unfamiliar with don't be afraid to experiment; they can be great to try if you fancy a change, or if you are simply bored with light or full-bodied dry whites.

Part of the charm of spicy wines is their sometimes over-the-top, very overt fragrance, and people either love or hate them. Try a bottle out on a group of friends and you'll see what I mean. They are certainly conversation enhancing!

The majority of wines in this section are produced in France's Alsace region, an area which has changed nationality so many times over the years that many people today still think of it as part of Germany rather than northern France.

The towns certainly look Germanic with their timber-framed houses and narrow streets. The food served in the local restaurants is German in style, and you'll even hear German spoken. But the wines are definitely French in character, and are dry, with depth, complexity and a unique

Alsatian character. In fact, one could go as far as to say that no Bootful should be without its Alsatian!

In this section, you'll notice that the list of grape variety abbreviations is very different. This is because many of Alsace's top varieties are rarely found elsewhere in France. As you'll see, they are a very spicy collection indeed.

The richest, most luscious wines – produced from any of these grape varieties – are known as Vendange Tardives or 'late harvest' wines. This is not because the grapes are harvested late into the night (a good time to enjoy this wine, perhaps) but because they are brought in so late in the season – as late as December following a standard September or October harvest.

Vendange Tardives have deliberately been included in this section, rather than the chapter on sweet whites, as they actually cover a wide range of styles: predominantly spicy, but varying from medium dry to seriously rich and luscious. Contrary to popular opinion they are not always super sweet in taste. At their most opulent, they are deliciously rich, sticky and full of intense tropical sweet fruit, finishing with a refreshing tang of acidity which prevents them from tasting cloying.

Apart from Alsace wines there are some other spicy oddballs to try, particularly Jurançon from the southwest of France, and Montlouis from the Touraine region of the Loire Valley.

As well as being an unusual aperitif (a glass of chilled, dry, flowery Muscat always goes down well on a sunny day in the garden), spicy wine is wonderful with food. If you cannot think of a wine to go with a particular dish, there is a good chance that one from this section will rise to the occasion.

Because of their intensity of flavour and overt

spiciness, many can be excellent foils for highly flavoured spicy food. Try a Gewurztraminer with aromatic Thai cooking; its tropical flavours are a more than adequate match for those of lemon grass, chilli, lime leaves and coconut. The grapey, almost marmalade-like character of both Muscat and Jurançon complements the sweet and sour flavours of Chinese cooking too, especially dishes served with black bean or sweet plum (Hoi-Sin) sauce.

The richer, more luscious wines of this style will go well with puddings, especially if you like the dry, citrus-like tang of acidity they have on the finish. They can transform a pudding of fresh fruit into a much more tasty and memorable treat!

The Wines

KEY TO GRAPE VARIETY ABBREVIATIONS
  CB   Chenin Blanc
  Gew Gewurztraminer
  Mu   Muscat
  Ries   Riesling
  Syl   Sylvaner
  Tok   Tokay
  Mxd   Mixed

Edelswicker   AC   Mxd   F
(*ed-ells-vick-er*)

The cheapest of all Alsace wines, made from a blend of grapes grown on the low quality plains. Many people look down on this wine, but, for an ultra-cheap, spicy white, it takes some beating.

Despite contempt, most Alsace producers make an Edelzwicker; you'll need to taste few to see whose you prefer.

See 'Gewurztraminer d'Alsace' (below) for recommended producers.

Gaillac (*guy-ack*) AC Mxd F

Produced in southwest France, Gaillac whites are fresh and fruity. They have a touch of apparent sweetness gained from the floweriness of the grapes used to make them: Sauvignon Blanc mixed with Mauzac, Muscadelle, Sémillon and other varieties. They are grapey, with an almost peachy aroma (from the Muscadelle grape) and medium dry fruit, and are best drunk young.

Gaillacs with the word '*doux*' on the label are the fully blown sweet wines.

Good producers include Domaine de Gradde, Cave de Labastide de Levis, Mas Pignou, Cave Coopérative de Tecou.

Gewurztraminer d'Alsace AC Gew FF–FFF
(*gev-urrt-stram-inner dall-sass*)

Gewurztraminer is the spiciest grape variety of all. It produces one of Alsace's most unusual and distinctive wines; one which many growers around the world have tried to copy.

A sniff of this is like sticking your nose into a bowl of tropical fruit salad to which a sprinkle of cinnamon has been added: all that fruit flavour is carried through from the aroma to the palate, and yet, despite all the apparent sweetness, the wine actually tastes dry.

Vendange Tardives (late harvest wines – *see* the introduction to this section) are the richest and spiciest Gewurztraminers of the lot, with masses of mouth-filling fruit, and a flavour that lingers for ages. They are intensely sweet, with wonderful richness; you need to be rich to buy them too, as they are extremely expensive.

Be warned though, Gewurztraminer is a grape you'll either love or hate – there is no half-way house. Taste it before loading your Bootful!

Recommended producers: Becker, Beyer, Blanck, Cattin, Dopff & Irion, Dopff au Moulin, Rolly Gassmann, Maison Louis Gisselbrecht, Willy Gisselbrecht, Hugel, Marc Kreydenweiss, Preiss-Zimmer, Schlumberger, Trimbach and Zind-Humbrecht.

Jurançon	AC	Mxd	F–FF
(*sjure-on-sonn*)			

This is made in southwest France around Pau, from the unusual Petit and Gros Manseng grapes. It is a very individual wine, with an aroma of cinnamon mixed with currants and ginger, and lots of zippy, tangy, fruity flavours reminiscent of spiced pineapples and star fruit. A citrus kick of acidity on the finish accentuates spicy fruit flavour that lingers too.

An oddity for the Bootful, and probably best bought in small quantities unless you are certain you really like the unusual taste. Wines with the word '*sec*' on the label are drier and less exotic tasting (*see* pages 70–71 for Jurançon Sec).

Recommended producers include the Cave Coopérative de Gran-Jurançon.

Montlouis (*mon-loo-ee*)	AC	CB	FF

An oddity from the Touraine region of the Loire Valley. It is made from the chameleon-like Chenin Blanc grape, which makes wines of every style, from very dry right through to very sweet: this one lands in the middle.

Montlouis wines have a lightly honeyed aroma, a slightly peachy, earthy fruit flavour (with hints of lychees), and zippy acidity on the finish. They do, however, vary a lot from producer to producer, so make sure you taste some before buying any in large quantities.

Recommended producers include Berger, Deletang, and Levasseur.

| **Muscat d'Alsace** | AC | Mu | FF–FFF |
| *(moose-car dall-sass)* | | | |

If Gewurztraminer is the spiciest grape of them all, then Muscat is the grapiest. It has a highly perfumed aroma with a hint of roses and lots of wonderful grapey and strawberry flavours. On first tasting this wine you imagine it will finish sweet, but an unexpected refreshing tang of acidity cuts through the sweetness and it in fact it ends up quite dry. The only exception to this will be in the rare Vendange Tardive wines (Vendange Tardive will appear on the label), which have been harvested late and are intensely sweet and very expensive.

Muscat d'Alsace is a great wine to drink when you want something different and are fed up with standard dry whites.

GRAPE VARIETIES FOR **MEDIUM-DRY & SPICY WHITES**	**PRICE CODE**
CB Chenin Blanc	F Cheap: less than 20 francs a bottle.
Gew Gewurztraminer	
Mu Muscat	FF Medium: 20–70 francs a bottle.
Ries Riesling	
Syl Sylvaner	FFF Expensive: more than 70 francs a bottle.
Tok Tokay	
Mxd Mixed	

See 'Gewurztraminer d'Alsace' (pages 95–96) for recommended producers.

Pinot Gris d'Alsace   AC   Tok   FF–FFF
(*pee-no gree dall-sass*)

The same wine as Tokay d'Alsace. *See opposite*.

Riesling d'Alsace   AC   Ries   FF–FFF
(*reece-ling dall-sass*)

This is a wine with a distinctly petrolly aroma and, like many wines from Alsace, can smell as if it's going to be very sweet when it is in fact bone dry. Riesling develops amazingly in the bottle and tasting one when young and fairly acidic in no way prepares you for the rich, oily lusciousness it can develop in later years.

Alsace growers consider Riesling their most stylish wine, so it is often their most expensive. The most pricey, and luscious, are the Vendange Tardives.

See 'Gewurztraminer d'Alsace' (pages 95–96) for recommended producers.

Savennières   AC   CB   FFF
(*savv-enn ee-air*)

This delicious oddball wine comes from the Anjou-Saumur region of the Loire Valley. There the grapes (Chenin Blanc) grow on south-facing vineyard slopes on the river's north bank, where they get the maximum possible sunshine, and are able to achieve their fullest ripeness.

Savennières is much richer and more complex than the average dry Anjou or white Saumur. And while dry, it has a strange, honeyed aroma, with a slightly tropical edge; its fruit character, when tasted young, seems dry, but as the wine matures gets gradually richer.

It's worth buying a few bottles and tucking them away to try in a few years time. But, because of their rarity, these wines are not cheap, and are hardly good material for the Bootful.

Good producers to look out for are Coulée du Serrant, Roche-aux-Moines and Clos du Papillon.

Sylvaner d'Alsace   AC   Syl   F–FF
(*sill-var-ner dall-sass*)

Sylvaner is an attractive, fragrant grape, which produces easy-drinking, zippy wine with a hint of spiciness rather than masses of it. It can be enjoyed young as it has lots of lively, earthy, appley fruit.

People tend to like Sylvaner d'Alsace, and, as it's never very expensive, one from a good producer is definitely affordable for the Bootful.

See 'Gewurztraminer d'Alsace' (pages 95–96) for recommended growers.

Tokay d'Alsace   AC   Tok   FF–FFF
(*tock-eye dall-sass*)

Tokay is often labelled Tokay-Pinot Gris; its style too takes several different guises. At its simplest, it is lightly spicy with a sort of soft, banana-like aroma, and a fruity, dryish flavour. And at its best as Vendange Tardive (*see* the introduction to this section), it is gloriously perfumed, rich, lusciously sweet and expensive. Tokay can be a good Bootful wine, depending its price and your taste.

See 'Gewurztraminer d'Alsace' (pages 95–96) for recommended producers.

– CHAPTER 10 –

SWEET WHITES

This is the lusciously sweet, sticky section of the book. And these are often referred to as dessert, or pudding wines because in Britain they are traditionally drunk at the end of a meal. Indeed, many of them are so rich they are like meals in themselves.

In France, however, sweet wines are often drunk as aperitifs, always very cold. If you go into a French bar you will often see the locals drinking them in the same way as dry or medium white wines would be drunk in Britain. I find them a refreshing change from the standard gin and tonic or dry white wine.

In the Sauternes region of Bordeaux, the classic combination is a glass of chilled Sauternes with *foie gras* at the beginning of the meal, and possibly a glass with the Rocquefort at the end. Blue cheese and sweet wine might seem like a strange idea, but they actually work very well together, the acidity of the cheese being balanced by the sweetness of the wine.

One of the great things about sweet wines is that, because they are so rich, a bottle can serve up to 12 people at the end of a meal. Many are also sold in half bottles which can be very useful too.

Those who think of this type of wine as being cheap and cloying may well be surprised. Sweet wines produced at the most basic level <u>are</u> generally very unpleasant and synthetic-tasting, but the best of the *appellation contrôlée* wines have great complexity, with layers of different flavours balanced by a refreshing tang of acidity. No Bootful should be without some of these golden delights!

Most French sweet wines are made by leaving the grape crop on the vines until long after it would normally have been harvested. This results in grapes which have accumulated very high levels of natural sugar, too much for the yeast to ferment into alcohol: it therefore stays in the wine, making it sweet. Most sweet wines nevertheless have a fairly high natural alcohol level, and some (Muscat de Beaumes-de-Venise, for example) have extra added so that they become a similar strength to port.

Sauternes, the world's most famous sweet wine, starts life like many other sweet wines, the grapes being left on the vines long after other producers have harvested their crops. However, in Sauternes the grapes are left on the vines even longer, and they are allowed to become infected with a type of rot known as 'noble rot' or *Botrytis cinerea*, which causes them to shrivel and turn into a horrid-looking brown sticky mess, resembling mouldy old currants.

It is only at this stage that the grapes are brought in. Much of their water content has evaporated and their natural sugar has become very concentrated indeed. The yields produced by grapes like this are understandably very low. And while producers have to endure all sorts of other (unwanted) rots every year, noble rot does not always appear: only when the climatic conditions are right – foggy mornings with sunshine breaking through around lunchtime – does botrytis set in.

So, low yields and dependence on such odd weather patterns mean that grapes good enough to make Sauternes are very hard to come by. This is one of the reasons why quality sweet wines will never be cheap and therefore may not feature as strongly in the Bootful as one would like. But while Sauternes is the most famous dessert wine, there are other regions in France producing sweet wines in similar ways for much cheaper prices – Coteaux du Layon and Vouvray from the Loire Valley to name just two.

Another method of producing sweet wines is to fortify the fermenting grape must with alcohol. This stops the fermentation mid-way, thus leaving unconverted grape sugar in the wine to make it sweet. Known in France as *vins doux naturel* (a strange term for wines which are not naturally sweet) these fortified wines certainly do fortify you as they are higher in alcohol than standard table wines with around 15%, or more.

France's best known *vin doux naturel* is Muscat de Beaumes-de-Venise, which suddenly shot up in price as it became fashionable about ten years ago when one of Britain's top supermarkets treated it to a major marketing campaign. Better bargains can be found in other similar wines like Rivesaltes.

Sweet wines are traditionally served with desserts or puddings and writing about them makes my mouth water! The trick to matching sweet wines and puddings is to ensure that the wine is sweeter than the food accompanying it. Otherwise, after one mouthful, the wine will taste dry. This is why it can be a little tricky matching a sweet wine with chocolate, though something as sweet and treacly as Banyuls would probably do the trick.

Whenever you drink sweet wine, always ensure the bottle is well chilled.

The Wines

KEY TO GRAPE VARIETY ABBREVIATIONS
CB   Chenin Blanc
Mu   Muscat
Sém/SB   Sémillon/Sauvignon Blanc blend
Mxd   Mixed

Banyuls   AC   Mxd   F–FF
(*bann-yoll*)

When visiting the Banyuls vineyards it helps to
have a head for heights – they are perched on the
edges of steep cliffs, precariously overhanging the
Mediterranean. The land is so rocky that it looks
unsuitable for growing anything at all, and growers
regularly lose their soil, vines and grapes over the
edge of the cliffs in violent winds or storms. Nevertheless, the vines flourish there, not far from Spain's
northeast border, along the edge of the Pyrenees,
making this France's most southerly appellation.

Banyuls is made from a mixture of grapes including Grenache and Muscat. It is a fortified wine – a
vin doux natural (*see* the introduction to this
section) – and is therefore more alcoholic than
standard table wine. Amber in colour, with ruby
tints, it has a particularly unusual character: an
aroma of almonds, marmalade and toasted fruit on
the palate, tinged with a touch of chocolate and
plum jam on the finish, rather like a tawny port.
While sweet, it is the added nuances of other
flavours which stop this wine from tasting cloying.

Wines named 'Grand Cru' are the ones which
have been aged in wood and have an even more
roasted and concentrated almondy flavour.

Drink Banyuls chilled, either with very rich puddings, especially chocolate and coffee flavoured, or fruit cake. The locals often enjoy it as an aperitif.

Barsac	AC	Sém/SB	F–FFF
(*bar-sack*)			

This is one of the villages (or communes) found within the Sauternes appellation allowed to use its own name on the label. It too produces sweet wine from grapes infected with noble rot (*see* the introduction page 101). Winemakers generally also add some Muscadelle to the traditional blend of Sauvignon Blanc and Sémillon grapes, as this gives an extra floweriness to the wine.

Luscious and rich, the best Barsacs combine fruity, slightly nutty aromas with lots of honeyed luxurious fruit on the palate and a tang of acidity on the finish. Very similar to Sauternes, purists argue that this is a marginally drier wine – it certainly has a more lemony flavour.

Because yields are so low, this type of wine can be very expensive, especially when produced by the more famous châteaux. And while a small amount is sold simply as 'Barsac' (worth the buy if it's cheap enough), most is sold under its château name and commands a hefty price. Sadly, this is not really Bootful material.

Recommended châteaux: Climens, Coutet, Doisy-Daëne, Doisy-Védrines, Liot, Nairac and Roumieu.

Bonnezeaux	AC	CB	FF–FFF
(*bonn-eh-zo*)			

Produced in the Anjou-Saumur district of France's Loire Valley, this is classy sweet wine; a far cry from the region's popular Anjou Rosé.

Bonnezeaux is made in a similar way to Sauternes (*see* page 101), from the classic white grape of the Loire, Chenin Blanc. It is rich and honeyed in character, with a slightly nutty aroma; ultra-sweet, yet also with a tang of acidity on the finish, which means it can be matured for many years.

There are still some bargain Bonnezeaux bottles to be found in the 'medium' price bracket as outside the Loire this wine is not widely known.

Cadillac (*cad-ee-ack*) AC Sém/SB F–FF

No, not an American stretch limousine; a little-known pudding wine which can be just as exciting.

Produced in Bordeaux, north of the river Garonne and Sauternes, the town of the same name is also well worth a visit: its architecture is as impressive as its wines, and inside its ancient walls the main tourist attraction is its attractive 17th-century château.

The grapes used for Cadillac are the same as those for Sauternes, and the wines are made in roughly the same way too, although yields are much higher and less emphasis is placed on their developing full-blown noble rot. As a result, Cadillacs are much lighter wines, the best, floral and sweet with good flavour, but without the intense lusciousness of their great (and much more expensive) Sauternes cousins.

GRAPE VARIETIES FOR SWEET WHITE WINES		PRICE CODE	
CB	Chenin Blanc	F	Cheap: less than 20 francs a bottle.
Mu	Muscat	FF	Medium: 20–70 francs a bottle.
Sém/SB	Sémillon/Sauvignon Blanc blend	FFF	Expensive: more than 70 francs a bottle.
Mxd	Mixed		

If you find a good Cadillac that is to your taste make sure you fit it in your Bootful and drive it home!

Coteaux du Layon   AC   CB   F–FF
(*cot-oh dew lay-on*)

Good value Bootful wines are produced in this part of the Loire Valley's Anjou-Saumur district. Made from the versatile Chenin Blanc grape, they vary from medium-sweet to those which are lusciously so and have been made from nobly rotten grapes (noble rot is explained in the introduction to this chapter – *see* page 101).

Quality varies greatly from year to year, but as a general rule the hotter the summer, the better will be the wines are that are produced.

Because of their good acidity, Coteaux du Layon can be laid down and matured for years. Then they become richer in colour, and take on delicious nutty aromas and flavours with hints of molasses. But the wines have enough charm to be enjoyed young too. They are one of the best finds of the Loire Valley; don't miss them!

Graves Supérieure   AC   Sém/SB   F
(*grahv soop-air-ee-er*)

Today Bordeaux's Graves region is best known for its production of red and dry white wines; but 20 years ago it was far more usual to see the sweet white Graves wines entitled to this appellation, which were sold all around the world.

Graves Supérieures remain good value though, and if you experiment, some very pleasant ones can be found. The same grapes are used as for Sauternes and Barsac, and while these wines are a lot lighter in style, they are appealingly sweet, with lightly perfumed, floral undertones.

Loupiac (*loo-pee-ack*)   AC   Sém/SB   F–FF

Not a widely known appellation and therefore potentially a brilliant Bootful wine because its price can be very attractive.

Situated in the Bordeaux region to the north of Barsac, but on the opposite side (east) of the river Garonne, Loupiac makes pleasant, easy-drinking pudding wines. In common with all the sweet wines made in the area, Sémillon and Sauvignon Blanc grape varieties are mainly used, with a small amount of Muscadelle added for some extra spiciness.

Loupiac tends to be much lighter than the better known sweet wines from the region like Sauternes, though in good years it shows evidence of noble rot and an attractive richness on the palate. If you are fond of sweet wines, Loupiac is definitely worth checking out.

Monbazillac   AC   Sém/SB   F–FF
(*mon-baz-ee-ack*)

A great value sweetie from an appellation within the Bergerac region (to the east of Bordeaux), this wine is like mini-Sauternes, but sold at a fraction of the price.

Monbazillac often has a slightly honeyed aroma with a hint of coconut on the palate, and lots of lusciously sweet, yet tangy, citrus-like fruit. A good value Bootful contender.

Recommended producers include the *cave co-opérative*, which is based at Château de Monbazillac.

Muscat de Beaumes-de-Venise   AC   Mu   FF
(*moose-car de bome der venn-ease*)

Grown south of Rasteau in the Rhône Valley, this is still the most fashionable Muscat produced in France. It used to be extremely good value, but its popularity got the better of it and it is becoming increasingly expensive. Regardless of cost, however, it is a delicious fortified wine with an intense aroma of ripe grapes mixed with fresh raspberries.

Quality and price vary enormously from producer to producer, so make sure you know what you are buying. Those recommended include Domaine de Durban, Jaboulet and the *cave coopérative*.

Muscat de St-Jean de Minervois   AC   Mu   F
(*moose-car der san sjohn der min-airve-wah*)

This tropical, grapey, sweet wine can be just as good as Muscat de Beaumes-de-Venise (*see above*) but because it was never 'discovered' as such, it is much better value, and therefore better Bootful material. It comes from the Minervois region, where the vineyards flourish high above the sea.

This too is a *vin doux naturel* (a fortified wine), smelling very grapey, with a distinctive aroma and flavour of lychees and peaches. If you like the over-the-top flavour of the Muscat grape, this is the wine for you. Make sure you drink it very chilled.

Pineau des Charentes   AC   Mxd   F
(*peen-oh day shar-ont*)

This is a wine you'll either love or hate, so make sure you taste it before loading your Bootful! The fact that it is produced in the Cognac region gives a good clue as to its style. Made from a blend of grapes including Ugni Blanc, Colombard and Sémillon, cognac is added to the juice before all the grape sugar has been fermented out, resulting in a sweet fortified wine.

The locals tend to drink it as an aperitif rather than as a pudding wine, sometimes even mixed with tonic to make a longer drink. Its full, grapey aroma is followed by a sort of sweet, almost musty, but quite dense fruity taste, topped with a hint of vanilla from the oak casks in which it is aged.

It does not carry a vintage but wines with the words 'Vieux Pineau' on their label will have been aged for at least five years and will have a much richer, more nutty aroma. If you do like drinking this as an aperitif, be warned; it contains around 18% alcohol, much more than you might think.

Quarts de Chaume   AC   CB   F–FFF
(*car der shome*)

This is another relatively unknown, but great, sweet white from the Loire Valley, made in the Coteaux du Layon region. Its vineyards flourish around the village of Chaume, producing both medium sweet and sweet wines which can last for years.

Many wines which start off seeming relatively dry, actually become sweeter as they mature. The best Quarts de Chaumes have a rich, slightly

GRAPE VARIETIES FOR SWEET WHITE WINES		PRICE CODE	
CB	Chenin Blanc	F	Cheap: less than 20 francs a bottle.
Mu	Muscat		
Sém/SB	Sémillon/Sauvignon Blanc blend	FF	Medium: 20–70 francs a bottle.
Mxd	Mixed	FFF	Expensive: more than 70 francs a bottle.

peachy aroma and soft, honeyed fruit with a citrus tang on the finish – a bit like refined marmalade!

These wines go surprisingly well with river fish dishes like pike, especially those served with quite rich, creamy sauces.

Rivesaltes   AC   Mu   F–FF
(*reev-salt*)

Produced in the sunny south of France, along the coast south of Perpignan, this is another delicious fortified wine made from several different grape varieties, principally though, the Muscat and Grenache. The resulting wines vary in colour from light golden to an intense ruby red.

They display all sorts of marmalade-like characteristics, with several different aromas and a wonderful mish-mash of fruit tastes, all combining with a raisiny finish.

Those made just from the Muscat will generally state this on the label and tend to be more grapey and somewhat less raisiny in flavour.

Sainte-Croix-du-Mont   AC   Sém/SB   F–FF
(*sant c-wah der mon*)

Another lesser-known jewel in Bordeaux's crown, this luscious wine is produced alongside those of Loupiac and Cadillac, although this is much finer than the latter.

Similar to Sauternes and Barsac, Sainte-Croix-du-Monts are elegant, yet sweet and luscious, and can be extremely good value. They are definitely worth searching for and are good Bootful material. They will mature well if you can resist drinking them for long enough.

Sauternes (*so-tairn*) AC Sém/SB FF–FFF

This region is home to the most famous (and most expensive) sweet wine in the world, Château d'Yquem. Yquem is certainly not for your Bootful, and in fact very few Sauternes are. Believe it or not, you will be better off buying them in Britain!

All Sauternes are made from blends of Sémillon, Sauvignon and (sometimes) Muscadelle grapes. These are picked very late, when their natural sugar is at a very high level, and are encouraged to develop botrytis (noble rot). The incredibly small crops which result are the main reason for Sauternes' sky-high price. It's likely to remain high too, so if you see a cheap one, it can be well worth buying; but it is essential, if you do, to taste a bottle before investing in any quantity.

Recommended producers from Sauternes (and Bommes, a sub-district) include Châteaux Filhot, Guiraud, Lafaurie-Peyraguey, Lamothe-Guignard, Raymond-Lafon, Rayne-Vigneau, Rieussec, Sigalas-Rabaud, Suduiraut, La Tour-Blanche and d'Yquem.

Vouvray (*voo-vray*) AC CB F–FFF

One of the Loire Valley's most versatile wines, this can vary from very dry (sometimes sparkling) through to medium sweet, and to rich, luscious and very sweet. Sometimes producers are not overly helpful and don't indicate which style their wine is.

But if you see the word '*moelleux*', you can be sure that the wine will have a rich, honeyed, elder-flower-like aroma and ripe, lusciously sweet fruit on the palate. The best will last for years.

Recommended producers include Clos Baudoin, Brédif, Huet and Château Montcontour.

CHAPTER 11

LIGHT REDS

If you have ever enjoyed a bottle of beaujolais, the chances are that you like light red wines. They are easy to drink, with a refreshing tang of acidity, and none of the bitter tannin found in medium-bodied reds and young clarets. Being light, not full-bodied, they are often deliciously fruity and thirst-quenching.

Try an experiment. Offer a glass of one, chilled, to a friend and ask them to taste it with their eyes closed. Then ask them to tell you what colour it is. The answer may surprise you. Many light reds actually taste like white wine because of their similar fruit, acidity and tannin. This makes them great for people who normally dislike reds, and also excellent aperitifs or party wines too as they are so gluggable.

In France, light reds are often drunk chilled, or even diluted with water and ice to make a longer drink. Forget the old adage that reds should be drunk at room temperature. This misleading saying was invented well before the advent of central heating, when room temperature was pretty chilly!

Many wines in this section are made from the Beaujolais grape, the gulpable Gamay – a grape whose popularity is spreading amongst France's vignerons and which many regions, particularly in the south, are beginning to plant (*see* pages 37–38 for its vital statistics). The other predominating variety is Cabernet Franc: an intensely fruity grape which is low in tannin. Again, delicious drunk chilled.

So when you are bored of dry whites but don't want the weight of a full red, try a light red wine. They make a welcome change, and they go very well with food too, equally complementary to roast chicken and turkey, and delicious with light white fish like plaice. Or enjoy them with cold meats and sausages, or pasta and salad dishes.

Many light reds even survive the challenge of chilli-laced, spicy food as the crisp acidity and fruit of the wine is able to cut through all its fiery hot flavours. A good glass can turn even the most ordinary meal, like bangers and mash, beans on toast, or even a sandwich, into a much more enjoyable event.

Served chilled at parties, picnics and barbecues, you'll soon discover your guests are finding them very more-ish. So they are definitely worth a Bootful.

If you are surprised not to find the top Beaujolais Crus (Fleurie, Juliénas, Morgon, etc) in this section, it is because they are more weighty than standard AC Beaujolais or Beaujolais-Villages, and are included in the Medium-Bodied Reds style section.

The Wines

KEY TO GRAPE VARIETY ABBREVIATIONS
Gam	Gamay
PN	Pinot Noir
Mxd	Mixed

Anjou (*on-sjoo*)   AC   Mxd   F

Mention the word Anjou, and everyone automatically thinks of medium-sweet Anjou Rosé. But this attractive region of the Loire Valley also produces some much better quality and less well-known (therefore keenly priced) reds.

The Anjou appellation covers the vineyards of Saumur, where the Cabernet Franc grape variety predominates for red wines; Cabernet Sauvignon is sometimes blended in too. While these two grapes produce medium- to full-bodied wines in many other areas, here they usually make light wines, with lots of red fruit flavours and little noticeable tannin. Locals often drink them chilled and particuraly enjoy them as an accompaniment to river fish.

Wines labelled Cabernet d'Anjou are not red, but rosé (*see* the Rosé style section, pages 178–185).

Gamay, the gulpable Beaujolais grape, is also grown in Anjou, and wines made entirely from it are sold as Gamay d'Anjou. They taste like light, slightly earthy versions of beaujolais, and are excellent value for money; ideal for the Bootful!

Ardèche (*ar-desh*)	VDP	Gam	F

This is a great Bootful red produced in the Ardèche region, to the south of the sunny Rhône Valley.

Several red grapes grow here, but the best by far is the fruity Gamay. The wines reflect plenty of its typical bubble-gum flavours – the ones found in beaujolais (*see below*) – but are slightly lighter than their popular cousin, though with just as much juicy fruit and tangy acidity. Ardèche reds are easy, every-day-drinking wines, and should be drunk young and chilled. So buy the most recent vintage available.

Beaujolais (*bo-sjol-ay*)	AC	Gam	F–FF

Because beaujolais is such fun, and has had such great publicity, it has been responsible for introducing many people to red wine. Its greatest asset is that, while being very fruity, it is not bitter and tannic and so is wonderfully drinkable even when young. It is ideal for everyday or party drinking, characterised by an abundance of bubble-gum flavours that appeal to most tastes.

Beaujolais Nouveau was originally invented as a brilliant marketing exercise too help speed up cash flow for the producers. Imagine their joy at banking the money for a wine just a month or so after their grapes were on the vines, rather than waiting the normal four month minimum!

If you are over in France when the Beaujolais Nouveau rush is on, be very careful which producers' wines you buy. The quality is very varied – the worst is disastrous, the best delicious. And don't ignore Beaujolais once the razzmatazz of Nouveau is over; it is an all year round wine and nearly always tastes better about six months after the harvest.

Producers worth looking out for include Chanut Frères, Duboeuf, Eventail de Producteurs, Ferraud, Jaffelin, Loron and Mommessin.

Beaujolais-Villages   AC   Gam   F–FF
(*bo-sjol-ay vee-larje*)

Full of fruit, these wines have slightly more body to them than standard beaujolais and are made in one or more of the 38 designated villages within the area of this appellation. The extra word 'Villages' on the label tends to add a few francs to the price though, so unless tried and tested, straightforward beaujolais is often a better Bootful bet.

These are rarely as full as the Beaujolais Cru wines (Fleurie, etc), which are found in the Medium-Bodied Reds style section, pages 120–164.

For recommended producers *see* Beaujolais, above.

Coteaux du Lyonnais   AC   Gam   F
(*cot-oh dew lee-onn-ay*)

Sandwiched between Beaujolais to the north and the Côtes du Rhône to the south, this region produces easy-drinking, fruity, bubble-gum flavoured light reds from the Beaujolais grape, Gamay. Although little known in Britain, wines have been produced in this region since Roman times. Locals enjoy them chilled. Not widely found in supermarkets, but nonetheless excellent Bootful material.

Coteaux Varois   VDQS   Mxd   F
(*cot-oh var-wah*)

Holiday-makers drink this one by the gallon while sun-seeking in the south of France's Provence region. Take a good sniff of it and the ripe grapes and lightly-burnt curranty aromas instantly conjure up long sunny days, warm balmy evenings, and lots of deliciously garlicky Provençale food.

All sorts of grapes are blended together to make Coteaux Varois, including many which are used in the Côtes du Rhône: Grenache, Cinsaut, Mourvèdre and Syrah, together with Carignan and sometimes a dash of Cabernet Sauvignon. The wines vary between light- and medium-bodied, and are certainly good Bootful material, especially if their rather rustic, raisiny flavour is to your taste. (They are often better chilled!)

Côtes du Tarn   VDP   Gam   F
(*coat dew tarn*)

This *vin de pays* region produces varying styles of red wine. The tastiest, and the only one which really falls into this style section, is made from the famous Gamay grape. It is an easy-drinking wine with less acidity than beaujolais (from Gamay too) and a particularly attractive aroma of violets.

The other red produced is a much more full-bodied and robust wine, more akin to a slightly lighter Cahors (*see* page 167) from the region which lies to the north of this one. Cabernet Sauvignon and Cabernet Franc, together with Syrah and Merlot as well as some local varieties, are used this time.

Gaillac (*guy-ack*)	AC	Mxd	F

From southwest of Cahors, the red wines of Gaillac are made from a blend of grapes which includes gulpable Gamay, Duras, Syrah, Cabernet Sauvignon and Cabernet Franc. They are made using the same techniques as for beaujolais, producing delicious lightish wines with flavours reminiscent of light Bordeaux or Rhônes, and hints of beaujolais too: a combination of simple fruitiness with an underlying, slightly earthy flavour. Certainly a good Bootful wine. Ideal drunk chilled at summer parties.

Jardin de la France (*jar-dan der la fronce*)	VDP	Gam	F

This huge *vin de pays* area encompasses wines from all over the Loire Valley, an area best known

GRAPE VARIETIES FOR LIGHT RED WINES		**PRICE CODE**
Gam	Gamay	F Cheap: less than 20 francs a bottle.
PN	Pinot Noir	FF Medium: 20–70 francs a bottle.
Mxd	Mixed	FFF Expensive: more than 70 francs a bottle.

for its range of white wines. But the reds, a better kept secret, are better value too, and definitely good for stocking up your Bootful!

Some of the best, most fruity light reds of this region are made from the Gamay grape, and have lots of ripe character and quite soft acidity. Others you'll find are made from the earthy, red fruit flavoured Cabernet Franc, so look carefully at the labels to see if there is any indication of which variety has been used.

Marsannay (*mar-sann-ay*)　　AC　　PN　　F–FF

Although not widely seen in Britain, this red burgundy is found in many French supermarkets and is a definite bargain for the Bootful.

Produced in the north of the Côtes de Nuits, not far from the city of Dijon, this region has long had a good reputation for rosé wines. Recently, however, the reds have taken over some of the limelight. They are very fruity Pinot Noir wines, with lots of strawberry fruit flavour and a touch of spiciness on the finish. The overall impression is soft and rounded without any bitter tannin.

Recommended producers include Bruno Clair.

Pinot Noir d'Alsace　　　　　　AC　　PN　　FF
(*pee-no nwar dall-sass*)

Pinot Noir is the one black grape variety grown in the Alsace region. It produces wines there which often appear dark rosé in colour rather than red, although proud producers get rather offended if you point this out! Their flavour is delicious, complemented by a soft, earthy, raspberry-like aroma.

These are unusual wines, more easily available

in France than Britain, and I recommend including them in any Bootful as they are extremely versatile: ageing well for a few years, yet also enjoyable young and chilled.

Good producers include Beyer, Blanck, Dopff & Irion, Gisselbrecht, Hugel, Marc Kreydenweiss, Preiss-Zimmer, Rolly Gassmann, Schlumberger, Trimbach and Zind-Humbrecht.

St-Chinian   AC   Mxd   F
(*sann shin-ee-ann*)

Not widely known in Britain, but a good all rounder to include in your Bootful. Produced in the Languedoc-Roussillon region, these wines are light in colour but full of mouth-watering fruit nevertheless. They are made from a mixture of Cinsaut, Carignan, Grenache, Mourvèdre and Syrah, and are rather like light, but more elegant wine from the Côtes du Rhône.

Recommended producers include the Cave Coopérative de Roquebrun.

Touraine (*too-rain*)   AC   Gam   F

A red winner from the Loire Valley. The best wines in this appellation are made from the fruity Gamay grape, whose name will often appear on the label as 'Gamay de Touraine'. Full of juicy fruit these are anytime-drinking wines, guaranteed to please most who try them. And like all the Loire reds, they can be enjoyed chilled.

Touraine wines tend to have a little more class than Gamay sold as 'Jardin de la France' (*see* pages 117–18), and are good for the Bootful.

– CHAPTER 12 –

MEDIUM-BODIED REDS

Medium reds occupy the most space in this book, and if you have ever enjoyed a basic red Bordeaux or burgundy then you'll find this style section includes a great many delicious wines. The Bootful bargain hunter is positively spoiled for choice with such a wide range to select from.

This plentiful array reflects both French drinking habits and wine production – the exact opposites to those of the British. The French in fact drink two-thirds red wine to only one-third white.

Medium-bodied reds are made from almost every grape variety imaginable, from the soft, velvety Pinot Noir, to the tannic Cabernet Sauvignon (the classic claret grape) and the more spicy varieties like Syrah and Grenache grown in France's more southerly regions. There are hundreds of different flavours to be found and you are bound to discover several to suit both your palate and pocket.

The best value are often among the lesser known names, so don't be frightened to experiment as this is almost certainly where you'll find the Bootful bargains. If you have a well-known, but pricey favourite though, simply glance through the entries here to find a wine made from the same grapes. It is likely to have a family resemblance even if it is from a different area, perhaps one you haven't heard of, so it may be well worth giving a try.

Vins de pays (*see* page 21) are especially good value, particularly those produced in the south of France where quality is consistently high. Make sure you try those from Catalan, Collines Rhodaniennes, Comté Tolosan, Sables du Golfe du Lion and the aptly named Vallée du Paradis.

Among the Pinot Noir-based wines, look out especially for Bourgogne Rouge, Bourgogne Passe-tout-grains, Givry and Mercurey, all of which are much cheaper than Burgundy's more famous names like Gevrey-Chambertin or Beaune.

Bordeaux and Bordeaux-style bargains include Bergerac, Côtes de Bourg, Côtes de Buzet, Côtes de Duras and the *vins de pays* from the Dordogne. They are all lighter than the traditional top clarets, but are very attractive for drinking fairly young.

The spicy reds produced in the Rhône Valley are often great Bootful value too. Search out Côtes du Ventoux, Coteaux du Tricastin and Vacqueyras.

If you prefer reds with richer, overtly fruity juiciness, try a Beaujolais 'Cru' wine (there are just ten of them). It's best to buy the lesser known ones like Chénas and Chiroubles which are better value, rather than the well known names like Fleurie or St-Amour. Alternatively, the frank, red fruit flavoured Cabernet Franc wines produced in the Loire Valley, like Bourgueil and Chinon, can be delicious.

Medium-bodied reds are very pleasant to drink on their own as aperitifs (a custom more common in France than Britain). The French also drink them chilled, a sight which horrifies the wine snob, but they are actually very refreshing this way – I generally keep a few bottles of a light Beaujolais Cru or a southern *vin de pays* in my fridge at home.

All of them are excellent with food. Match the weight of the meal and the wine, serving medium-bodied reds with medium-flavoured foods. Serve them with all sorts of roast meats – beef, pork and lamb – and traditional British fare like steak and kidney pie or beef and Guiness pie. They are complementary too to wine-based dishes like Coq au Vin or Boeuf Bourgignonne.

Some of these wines, particularly Loire reds, go well with fish: river fish like pike and perch, or more fleshy sea fish like monkfish and turbot. All these dishes are delicious served with a red wine sauce.

Finally, the cheese course. Medium-bodied reds are great with cheese, especially good old English Cheddar, Cheshire and Double Gloucester.

Such a wide choice, and so many occasions when you can enjoy these wines, make them ideal candidates for your Bootful!

The Wines

KEY TO GRAPE VARIETY ABBREVIATIONS

CS	Cabernet Sauvignon
CF	Cabernet Franc
Gam	Gamay
Mer	Merlot
PN	Pinot Noir
Syr	Syrah
CS/Mer	Cabernet Sauvignon/Merlot blend
Mxd	Mixed

Aloxe-Corton AC PN FF–FFF
(*al-ox kor-tonn*)

Once seduced by good red burgundies like this, you are in trouble – they don't come cheap. Produced in the northern Côte de Beaune (which concentrates mostly on white wines) these are as good as many from the famous red wine villages of the Côte de Nuits (eg, Gevrey-Chambertin and Morey-St-Denis).

Good red burgundies can be enjoyed when young as they don't have the same quantities of bitter tannin that make young Bordeaux so undrink-able. But if you can resist them, they age well too.

Aloxe-Corton is made from Pinot Noir and shows all the grape's best characteristics: a soft, rasp-berry-like aroma, rich, very slightly sweet fruit on the palate, and soft earthiness on the finish.

Recommended producers include Bonneau du Martray, Chandon de Briailles, Dubreuil-Fontaine, Parent, Rapet, and Tollot-Beaut.

| **Anjou** (*on-sjoo*) | AC | CF | F |

Though famous for its often indifferent rosé, there are many interesting wine styles made in the Loire Valley's Anjou district. The reds (ranging from light to medium-bodied) are amongst some of the best value: wonderfully refreshing, great drunk chilled, and, if the locals' taste is anything to go by, go well with all sorts of river fish.

Wines with the words 'Cabernet d'Anjou' on the label are made from Cabernet Franc grapes. These have a delicious bouquet of red fruits which is carried through onto the palate and backed up with refreshing grassy, earthy flavours and a good tang of acidity. Because they are not too tannic, many people who normally dislike reds will enjoy these.

| **Aude** (*ode*) | VDP | Mxd | F |

Load your Bootful with these value-for-money southern reds – they are a tasty bargain! Produced in a large area of sunny Languedoc-Roussillon (southern France), these are wines enjoyed by many on holiday and which taste just as good back home.

Aude wines are designed to be glugged rather than talked about, and can be drunk either as they come, or chilled. They are made from a blend of local varieties including Carignan, Grenache, Cinsaut, Syrah, Merlot and Cabernet Sauvignon, and have a wonderful aroma of mixed red and black berries, with juicy underlying fruit and enough weight to go with garlicky, southern Provençale-style food – yet not too much bitter tannin so as to over power it. Aude wines are often available in larger bottles and bag-in-box.

Auxey-Duresses   AC   PN   FF–FFF
(*oak-see dure-ess*)

A wonderful red wine, which can still be good value as it is one of Burgundy's better kept secrets. Its vineyards are next to Meursault's (which produce red and white wine), but, perhaps because the name is more difficult to say, it is less often asked for.

Soft, with lots of ripe, raspberry-like fruit, this wine combines the aroma of fresh raspberry leaves with a soft, slightly oaky flavour. It's a great alternative to the more expensive, more famous, and often overrated, wines of the Côte d'Or.

Recommended growers: Ampeau, Coche-Debord, Diconne, Jaffelin, Leflaive, Leroy and Roulot.

Beaune (*bone*)   AC   PN   FF–FFF

Beaune is the historic walled city at the centre of one of the world's most prestigious wine regions – Burgundy. Its wines are amongst those of the Côte d'Or which, though famous, are often overrated.

At their best, they are incredible. Aged in new oak barrels, they can have a wonderful complexity of raspberries, vanilla, and even farmyards! The top ones (like Drouhin's Beaune Clos des Mouches) are mind-blowing. Sadly, the rest, which is most of them, are dull and over-priced. Not Bootful wines.

Recommended producers include Bouchard Père, Chantale-Lescure, Delagrange, Drouhin, Jadot, Jaffelin, Morey and Tollot-Beaut.

Bergerac   AC   Mer/CF   F–FF
(*bear-sjehr-ack*)

The same name as the television detective, this wine is a bargain find and a must for the Bootful.

Situated to the east of the city of Bordeaux, the Bergerac region produces red wines that are not only good value but some of the best in southwest France. They are similar in character to Bordeaux as they are made from the same grapes, a mixture of Merlot, Cabernet Franc and Cabernet Sauvignon. They combine smooth blackcurrant fruit with just the right amount of tannin and structure and are not too bitter or overpowering. Easy-drinking reds, good quality, and great on their own or with food.

Appellation Côtes de Bergerac wines are virtually the same, but if you look carefully at the label, you'll see they have an extra degree of alcohol.

Recommended producers include Château La Jaubertie (owned by Englishman Nick Ryman).

Bordeaux (*bore-doe*)   AC   CS/Mer   F–FF

Said to be the Englishman's favourite tipple, Bordeaux or 'claret', is one of the world's most famous red wines. Its appellation covers such a large area that all sorts of different qualities of wine are produced, varying from the ecstatic to the abysmal. Today, however, the best producers make great efforts to maintain quality, and the boring wines which were commonplace ten years ago are now seen less often.

Bordeaux wines vary in character, depending both on where in the region they are from and the winemaking techniques used. Their price can be an indicator of quality, although it is not always; and, in theory, château-bottled wines are of a higher standard than blends from several properties, but this too can never be guaranteed. It is really best to experiment. If you are on holiday in France, make sure you try lots of wines from this appellation, and note any which are particularly to your taste.

A good Bordeaux has body, lots of ripe fruit, and an attractive amount of balancing tannin which gives the wine structure. Claret in this price bracket can age for a few years, but is normally sold ready for drinking and so won't generally get any better after a year or two.

Bordeaux Supérieur   AC   Mer/CF   F–FF
(*bore-doe soup-air-ee-er*)

Often superior in quality, but always superior in price! In theory, these wines have an extra half a degree of alcohol and are richer than many standard Bordeaux (*see above*).

Many wines classified under this appellation will not be blends, but the produce of a single château which will be named on the label. Again, if on holiday in the Bordeaux region, try and experiment with a few of these to find which are to your taste before loading your Bootful.

Bourgogne   AC   PN   F–FF
(*bore-goyn-ya*)

The great thing about buying wine is that in order to get the best buys you have to keep doing your homework. So if, like me, you are fond of the soft, raspberry-like fruit of the Pinot Noir grape, experimenting to find a good Bourgogne Rouge (red burgundy) is no great hardship!

This red can come from vineyards anywhere within the Burgundy region, and so includes a whole host of wines of very varied quality. They can range in style too, from relatively light and earthy, to richer, slightly jammy, and much softer. Sometimes producers with the right to a higher appellation will declassify their wines to straight Bourgogne, so if you see one for sale with the name of a grower whose other more prestigious wines you have enjoyed, try it.

Most producers make a Bourgogne Rouge, so sample a few and select one whose style you like.

Bourgogne Passe-Tout-Grains   AC Gam/PN F–FF
(*bore-goyn-ya pass-too-grann*)

Rarely seen in British shops, this basic red burgundy is a regular contender in the French supermarket

GRAPE VARIETIES FOR MEDIUM-BODIED RED WINES		CS/Mer	Cabernet Sauvignon /Merlot blend
CS	Cabernet Sauvignon	**PRICE CODE**	
CF	Cabernet Franc	F	Cheap: less than 20 francs a bottle.
Gam	Gamay		
Mer	Merlot	FF	Medium: 20–70 francs a bottle.
PN	Pinot Noir		
Syr	Syrah	FFF	Expensive: more than 70 francs a bottle.
Mxd	Mixed		

line-up. It can be extremely good value for money, so if it is to your taste it will be an ideal candidate for the Bootful.

Unlike other reds in the region this is made from a blend of grapes, namely Pinot Noir and the juicy Beaujolais grape, Gamay. Originally it contained many more varieties (whatever the winemaker had hanging around), hence its name.

The result is a wine bursting with lots of strawberry flavours, with attractive, refreshing, earthy acidity making it delicious when chilled. It's a good party wine and an ideal base for red wine spritzers.

Bourgueil (*bor-goy-ee*)   AC   CF   FF

Many people know the Loire Valley for its quality white wines and tend to overlook its stylish reds. Bourgueil is in fact one of the stars of the Loire and is certainly a wine for the Bootful. It comes from the Touraine region, and lies on the opposite bank of the river to the regions' other major quality red wine producing area, Chinon (*see* page 132).

Classic Bourgueil wines have a distinctly grassy smell, rather like white Sancerre (*see* page 78), with the flavours and aromas of lots of red fruits too, balanced with a good tang of acidity. While these wines are delicious young, they also age well if you can resist drinking them. Locals often serve them chilled, and in summer, when you are bored of dry white, there is nothing more refreshing.

The finest wines of this appellation come from the village of St-Nicholas-de-Bourgueil, and tend to be even more full-bodied, concentrated, and of course, a bit more expensive!

As the quality overall is high in this region, most growers can be recommended.

Brouilly (*broo-ee*)　　　　　　AC　　Gam　　FF

One of the ten Beaujolais villages ('Crus') allowed to use its own name for its wine. Brouilly has all the beaujolais character and more. Indeed most Cru wines tend to have greater depth of fruit and complexity than straight beaujolais, whilst retaining that delicious gulpable Gamay flavour.

Each village has its own characteristics too, and Brouilly, the largest and most southern of them, makes relatively full-bodied yet, at the same time, delicate wines. Although some of the more northerly beaujolais like Fleurie or Juliénas can age well, Brouilly is best drunk within its first five years.

Recommended producers include Chanut, Duboeuf, Eventail de Producteurs, Ferraud, Fessy, Loron, Mommessin and Sarrau.

Canon-Fronsac　　　　　　AC　　Mer/CF　　FF
(*can-on fron-sack*)

This may be an area you haven't heard of, but if you are a claret lover it is one you should get to know. Canon-Fronsac is in the Libournais region of Bordeaux, to the west of the St-Emilion and Pomerol appellations, but on the same right bank of the river Dordogne.

The wines are similar to St-Emilion in style, and tend to mature much faster than those made on the other side of the river in the Médoc (ie, they're ready to drink when much younger). An attractive violet aroma and ripe, tobacco-like, spicy, curranty fruit flavour with a hint of chocolate makes them ideal Bootful candidates. And because the region is not yet fashionable there are still some sold at bargain prices.

Recommended producers include Châteaux Canon Moueix, Canon-de-Brem, Junayme, Mausse, Mazeris, Toumalin and Vrai-Canon-Boyer.

Catalan (*cat-a-lann*)	VDP	Mxd	F

The eagle-eyed bargain hunter after a good value Bootful should certainly watch out for this wine. The vineyards are to be found along the western Mediterranean coast, in the northeast of the Pyrénées-Orientales region – near Rivesaltes where the sticky sweet white wine is made (*see* page 110).

Catalan wines are bursting with rich fruit, gaining a whole jamboree of flavours from the mixture of grapes used to make them: Carignan, Grenache, Cinsaut, Syrah, Merlot and Cabernet Sauvignon. They are easy-drinking, anytime wines which rarely disappoint and seem to please all.

Chambertin (*shom-ber-tan*)	AC	PN	FFF

Thought by some to be the king of the red burgundies, this is a Grand Cru of Gevrey-Chambertin. This means its quality is better, and, of course, the price much higher.

Rich and ripe, with soft, velvety fruit, just one taste of a good producer's version of this wine and you will understand why it is so expensive. Unfortunately, not all producers make good Chambertin and you can end up paying serious money for very boring wine. Not really Bootful material unless you are seriously rich!

Also watch out for 'Chambertin', preceded by the words 'Charmes', 'Chapelle' or 'Mazis' – these are the very best.

Recommended producers include Drouhin-Laroze, Ponsot, Rebourseau, Roty, Rousseau, Tortochot.

Chambolle-Musigny   AC   PN   FFF
(*shom-boll muse-een-yee*)

One of the very best red burgundies from the Côte de Nuits. As with most burgundy, a wine with 'Premier Cru' (or '1er Cru') on the label is well worth searching out as it will be from the village's top vineyards. The finest wines will have fabulous rich, raspberry-flavoured, classic Pinot Noir fruit.

However, as with all good burgundies, buying one can be like Russian roulette: too many producers make rubbish, and unless you buy (and know) the best, you are likely to be disappointed.

Recommended producers include Roumier and de Vogüé.

Chassagne-Montrachet   AC   PN   FF–FFF
(*shass-ann monn-rash-ay*)

This well-known Burgundy village in the famous Côte de Beaune region is better known for its white wine than its red. However, surprisingly, much more red is produced, and it is often available in French supermarkets. If at the lower end of the 'FF' price bracket this can be a good value wine, but never pay a lot for it.

Chénas (*chay-nass*)   AC   Gam   FF

One of the ten Beaujolais 'Crus', with plenty of bubble-gum flavour and lots of mouthwatering fruit. Chénas is one of the less commonly seen ones – probably because it's the smallest – though its quality is just as good. It is a medium-bodied to full red, without the staying power of its neighbour, Moulin-à-Vent (*see* page 153), yet with delicious, elegant, rounded fruit.

The name Chénas is derived from the ring of oak trees that used to grow in the village. A name worth remembering, as the wines are good value and deserve a place in the Bootful.

Recommended producers include Chanut, Duboeuf, Eventail de Producteurs, Ferraud, Fessy, Loron, Mommessin and Sarrau.

Chinon (*she-nonn*) AC CF FF

A great value, very tasty red, produced in the Loire Valley's Touraine region from the earthy Cabernet Franc grape variety. An upfront, juicy, fruity wine. Close your eyes and take a whiff and you'd be forgiven for thinking its grassy aroma was that of a white grape. But on the palate, the ripe red berry flavour gives the game away. A good tang of acidity adds to this wine's wonderfully refreshing style.

Along with Bourgueil (*see* page 128), this is one of the Loire's great red wines. It is very more-ish, and delicious to drink young, yet can also mature well too: the fruit and acidity become softer and the wine more mellow with age. Drink it chilled and make sure it has a place in your Bootful.

The quality overall is high in this region, so most Chinon growers can be recommended.

Chiroubles (*she-roo-bl*) AC Gam FF

One of the ten Beaujolais 'Crus' (wines entitled to use their village name) which, like Chénas, is still good value as it is not as well known as some of

132

the others – neighbouring Fleurie for example.

Made from 100% Gamay, as all beaujolais are, this is possibly the finest of the Crus, with a flowery, yet delicate aroma, and elegant, juicy fruit on the palate. Reserve it a place in your Bootful provided the price is not too high.

Recommended producers include Chanut, Duboeuf, Eventail de Producteurs, Ferraud, Fessy, Loron, Mommessin and Sarrau.

Chorey-lès-Beaune   AC   PN   FF–FFF
(*shorry-lay-bone*)

Not widely seen in England, perhaps due to the difficult-looking name, but much more widely available in France, especially in its home region.

This burgundy comes from the northern part of the Côte de Beaune and at its best oozes hefty, chewy, plummy Pinot Noir flavours. Comparatively full-bodied for burgundy, this is one which should be drunk within eight years of its vintage.

A good one for your Bootful, if you can find it.

Recommended producers include Germain and Tollot-Beaut.

Clos Vougeot (*klo voo-sjoe*)   AC   PN   FFF

This is also known as 'Clos de Vougeot'. It is one of the most famous Grand Crus from Burgundy's Côte de Nuits, and is well-known because its vine-yard is totally enclosed by a wall, hence the name 'Clos'. Its fame also stems from the fact that there are over 80 different owners of vineyard plots in the Clos, so in theory over 80 different Clos Vougeots can be made every vintage. However, the quality of the wine rarely matches the prestige of its name, and more often than not you would be better off selecting other red burgundies.

Collines Rhodaniennes VDP Mxd F
(*koll-een ro-dann-ee-enn*)

Don't worry if you've never heard of this wine, give it some space in your Bootful anyway.

Produced from vineyards in the heart of the Rhône Valley, it is a great value red, which can be made from a blend of many grapes. However, the better wines are sold as single varietals. Look out for those with the grape variety Gamay named on the label; these taste like lesser beaujolais, slightly softer on bite and acidity.

Alternatively, search for those made from the spicy northern Rhône grape, Syrah, which are characterised by masses of plummy fruit and are real bargains.

Comté Tolosan VDP Mxd F
(*compt-ay tol-oh-sann*)

This weird-sounding wine is well worth becoming familiar with. It is produced in the Midi-Pyrenees region of southern France, next to the mountains, and alongside the border with Spain.

GRAPE VARIETIES FOR MEDIUM-BODIED RED WINES		CS/Mer	Cabernet Sauvignon /Merlot blend
CS	Cabernet Sauvignon	**PRICE CODE**	
CF	Cabernet Franc	F	Cheap: less than 20 francs a bottle.
Gam	Gamay		
Mer	Merlot	FF	Medium: 20–70 francs a bottle.
PN	Pinot Noir		
Syr	Syrah	FFF	Expensive: more than 70 francs a bottle.
Mxd	Mixed		

Comté Tolosan reds are made from a blend of local grapes which are mixed with Cabernet Sauvignon, Cabernet Franc and Merlot to produce jammy, Bordeaux-style wines tending towards the heavier side of medium-bodied. They are good value for the Bootful.

Corton (*corr-tonn*)　　　　　AC　　PN　　FFF

One of burgundy's most famous red wines, grown on the hill of Corton, right at the northerly edge of the Côte de Beaune. The wines are big, burly, and packed with dense Pinot Noir flavours. Although they can be drunk young, it is advisable not to open a bottle before it is ten years old.

It may be worth investing in some of these, and packing them in your Bootful for special occasions.

Recommended producers include Bonneau du Martray, Bouzereau, Dubreuil-Fontaine, Parent, Rapet and Senard.

Costières de Nîmes　　　　AC　　Mxd　　　F
(*coss-tee-air der neem*)

Still relatively unknown, Costières de Nîmes produces great Bootful material. It has recently been granted *appellation contrôlée* status, but fortunately for us this has not caused prices to rise too much.

The region runs from Nîmes, at the top of the Rhône estuary, right down almost to the beaches of the Mediterranean, a few miles north of the ancient walled town of Aigues-Mortes.

The wines are spicy, yet rounded, with lots of mid-weight fruit. They are easy-drinking, and great party wines.

Côte de Beaune — AC — PN — FF
(*coat der bone*)

This Burgundy appellation (not to be confused with the extensive Burgundy vineyard area of the same name, or with straight Beaune – *see* pages 124–25) includes wines from a small vineyard area around the town of Beaune itself, and also in the Montagne de Beaune. They have wonderfully elegant, yet concentrated, raspberry-like Pinot Noir flavours and are great to drink young and fresh.

Good producers include Marchard de Gramont.

Côte de Beaune-Villages — AC — PN — FF
(*coat de bone vee-large*)

These reds come from an area known predominantly for its production of delicious white wine, the southern half of Burgundy's Côte d'Or – a larger region than AC Côte de Beaune, producing wine of less quality. But at the lower end of the medium price bracket these reds can be good value Bootful material for those who like the Pinot Noir grape. At their best they are delightfully fresh and fruity, with soft, earthy, strawberry flavours.

Don't confuse these wines with those from the appellation Beaune, which are more expensive (*see* pages 124–25).

Côte de Brouilly — AC — Gam — FF
(*coat de broo-ee*)

A richer and fuller wine than Brouilly, but in a similar style (*see* entry for Brouilly on page 129). Côte de Brouilly is full of bubble-gum fruit, and has a certain amount of tannin too. It can be a good bet for the Bootful but only if you can find it first; this wine is not often seen.

Recommended producers include Chanut, Duboeuf, Eventail de Producteurs, Ferraud, Fessy, Loron, Mommessin and Sarrau.

Côte de Nuits-Villages　　　AC　　PN　　FF
(*coat de nwee vee-large*)

Firm and fruity, these reds can come from five villages in the northern half of Burgundy's Côte d'Or, the best known of which is Fixin. These are Pinot Noir wines which, when well made, hint at the greatest of the region's more expensive reds. If you are lucky enough to see some, give them a place in your Bootful as they are well worth trying.

Recommended producers include two well-known growers: Jayer-Gilles and Daniel Rion.

Coteaux du Languedoc　　　AC　　Mxd　　F
(*cot-oh dew longer-dock*)

You are unlikely to go wrong with these wines as their quality is very consistent. Produced in the Languedoc-Roussillon area of southern France, north of the Pyrenees, they are straightforward reds, with lots of sun-baked southern fruit. Whilst not exactly elegant wines, they go down very well with highly flavoured food.

Coteaux du Tricastin　　　AC　　Mxd　　F
(*cot-oh dew tree-kass-tan*)

Great value Bootful material from the sunny southern Rhône. These are often better quality and value for money than other, more familiar wines from the area, like Côtes du Rhône.

They are blended from classic southern Rhône grapes: Grenache, Cinsaut, Mourvèdre and Syrah, and are full of spiciness and soft fruitiness on the finish. These are easy-drinking, tasty, good all-round party reds.

Côtes de Bourg   AC   Mer/CF   F–FF
(*coat der boorg*)

Next to Blaye (*see* Premières Côtes de Blaye, pages 156–57), this is a good Bootful wine for all the same reasons: plenty of velvety, violety Merlot fruit. Bourg is much smaller than Blaye as a region, but makes more wine, and the best are a step up in quality terms. Those from a good Bourg vintage will happily age for five to ten years.

Recommended producers include Châteaux de Barbe, de Bousquet, Brule Secaille, Caruel, Croûte-Courpon, Les Heaumes, Mercier, Peychaud, Rouselle, Rousset, Tayac and de Thau.

Côtes de Buzet   AC   Mer/CF   F–FF
(*coat der boo-zay*)

A good boozy wine, just right for the Bootful, produced 80 miles southeast of Bordeaux. Years ago Côtes de Buzet used to be included in the Bordeaux appellation, but was then granted its own. It is made from the classic claret grapes and the quality is consistently impressive.

The cooperative, Vignerons Reunis des Côtes de Buzet, has made massive investments both in viti-culture and vinification equipment over the last decade or so, and their wines are now particularly good value; highly recommended.

Côtes de Castillon   AC   Mer/CF   F–FF
(*coat der cass-tee-yon*)

St-Emilion lovers take note of this name – it is a good one for the Bootful. Côtes de Castillon is a large area to the east of St-Emilion, producing similar style clarets, though normally a little softer and for enjoying when just two or three years old. Don't go mad and buy your Bootful blind though; whilst the best Castillon wines are delicious there are many you would not want in any quantity.

Recommended producers include Châteaux de Clotte, Lesacques, de Pitray, Robin and La Terrace.

Côtes de Duras   AC   Mer/CF   F–FF
(*coat der dure-ass*)

A good value appellation to the east of Bordeaux, just below Bergerac. All the classic claret grapes are used to make this quality red from the south-west. It can be enjoyed young or can be kept for a few years. Another one for the Bootful.

Recommended producers include Château Berticot, Domaine Las Brugues-Mau Michau, Domaine de Ferrant and Domaine de Laulan.

Côtes de Francs   AC   Mer/CS   FF
(*coat der fronk*)

A newish arrival on the claret scene, this appellation lies northeast of Côtes de Castillon, St-Emilion's neighbour. The best wines are well rounded and structured, with delicious rich, silky Merlot flavours. Great Bootful wines, if you can find them.

Recommended producers include Châteaux de Francs, La Prade and Puygueraud.

Côtes de Thau   VDP   Mxd   F
(*coat der toe*)

These vineyards lie practically on the beach, hugging the coast southwest of Montpellier, around the port of Sète. Originally, gallons of very cheap and nasty wine were produced in this area, much of which either joined the wine lake or was distilled. But today, quality has improved beyond recognition and the reds are now simple, easy-drinking, soft and cheap. They are ideal for a large party and therefore great Bootful material.

Most producers are reliable.

Côtes du Frontonnais   AC   Mxd   F
(*coat dew fron-tonn-ay*)

This is another good Bootful red from the south-west of France. The appellation lies about 60 miles south of Cahors, east of Gaillac, and the wines are made from local grapes blended in with Rhône and Bordeaux varieties. They actually taste like a mixture of these two classics, with good full fruit and a spicy, southern, ripe fruit flavour.

Recommended producers include Château Bel-Air, Domaine Caze, Domaine de la Colombière, Cave Coopérative Côtes-de-Fronton and Les Daubans.

Côtes du Lubéron   AC   Mxd   F–FF
(*coat dew loo-bare-onn*)

Côtes du Lubéron, which has recently been elevated to *appellation contrôlée* status, is in the southern Rhône, south of Côtes du Ventoux and north of Aix-en-Provence.

It produces rich, ripe reds; ideal for the Bootful

because of their appealing sun-baked curranty fruit character and firmness. Some of them will last for a number of years.

Already the wines of Château Val Joanis (the most famous of the appellation) have gained a formidable reputation, and the rest are likely to follow suit; buy now as they will not be as cheap for much longer.

Recommended producers include Château La Canorgue, Clos Murabeau and Château Val Joanis.

Côtes du Marmandais   AC   Mer/CF   F
(*coat dew marr-monn-day*)

Sixty miles southeast of Bordeaux, this appellation surrounds the little town of Marmande and produces great claret taste-alikes from the same grapes (Cabernet Sauvignon, Cabernet Franc, Merlot). They are soft, easy-drinking, and well worth giving some space in your Bootful.

Côtes du Rhône   AC   Mxd   F
(*coat dew rone*)

This well-known, easy-drinking red can come from vineyards anywhere in the Rhône Valley.

Wines produced on estates or with a château

GRAPE VARIETIES FOR MEDIUM-BODIED RED WINES

CS	Cabernet Sauvignon	
CF	Cabernet Franc	
Gam	Gamay	
Mer	Merlot	
PN	Pinot Noir	
Syr	Syrah	
Mxd	Mixed	

CS/Mer   Cabernet Sauvignon /Merlot blend

PRICE CODE

F	Cheap: less than 20 francs a bottle.
FF	Medium: 20–70 francs a bottle.
FFF	Expensive: more than 70 francs a bottle.

name tend to be slightly fuller-bodied than those blended by a *négociant*. Quality does vary greatly throughout the region, so try a selection before loading up. The best, however, are certainly good for the Bootful.

Recommended producers include various excellent *caves coopératives* (including the one at Rasteau), Paul Jaboulet Aîné, Chapoutier, Château de Fonsalette, Guigal and Domaine de la Renjardière. However, this is a mere selection of the many good producers in this area.

Côtes du Ventoux AC Mxd F
(*coat dew von-too*)

Produced in the southern Rhône, you can often get better value for money from this appellation than from the neighbouring Côtes du Rhône AC, simply because the name is less well known. The wines are still not widely heard of in Britain, but are well distributed throughout French supermarkets.

Côtes du Ventoux are full, fruity wines with lots of southern spiciness and sometimes a slightly gamey finish. Excellent Bootful wines.

Recommended growers include Cave Coopérative du Coteaux du Mont Ventoux, Domaine St-Croix, Paul Jaboulet Aîné and (especially) Vieille Ferme.

Côtes du Vivarais VDQS Mxd F
(*coat dew veev-array*)

A good, fruity, gutsy Bootful wine, produced in the southern Rhône near Coteaux du Tricastin (*see* pages 137–38). These have lots of warm southern spicy fruit without any bitter tannin. Easy to drink, very cheap, and ideal for parties.

Crozes-Hermitage	AC	Syr	FF

(*croze-air-mee-tarj*)

A northern Rhône area right next to the famous Hermitage appellation. The only grape grown is the spicy Syrah, the best quality classic Rhône variety.

Crozes-Hermitage is considerably cheaper than its better known neighbour, and can be fantastic value. Indeed, a top producer's Crozes-Hermitage is often much better than an indifferent Hermitage.

The wine itself reflects the spiciness of the grape used to make it, and goes well with quite fully-flavoured food. It is definitely for the Bootful as it can be such a bargain.

Recommended producers include Chapoutier, Chave, Guigal, Paul Jaboulet Aîné and Sorrel.

Dordogne	VDP	Mer/CF	F

(*door-doyn-ya*)

The Dordogne river runs through a large part of southwest France into the Gironde estuary at the town of Bordeaux – it gives its name to a region that is a very popular holiday haunt with the British. Good Bootful wine is produced here from vines grown near Bergerac: the reds are like mini Bordeaux, with lots of ripe, blackcurranty fruit and a dry finish. They are rarely seen in Britain, and are good value, so it's worth taking advantage of their relative obscurity.

Echezeaux (*esh-ezz-oh*)	AC	PN	FFF

A Grand Cru from the Burgundy village of Vosne-Romanée in the Côte de Nuits, Echezeaux can be one of the very finest burgundies made. As such a tiny amount is produced it is never cheap and there is always a tremendous world-wide demand.

It's difficult to describe the flavour of a good Echezeaux, but it is soft, sensuous, with subtle raspberry overtones and masses of flavour. The price prohibits it from being a Bootful wine, though it is a great treat for a special occasion.

Also look out for Grands Echezeaux from neigh-bouring vineyards. This is very similar to Echezeaux, but has even greater intensity and style.

Faugères (*foe-sjair*)	AC	Mxd	F

Hardly known in Britain, Faugères definitely deserves a place in the Bootful. It is from the Languedoc-Roussillon region to the north of Beziers, and is fairly heavy-weight (on the borderline of this and the Full-Bodied Reds style section) and has masses of flavour. Made from spicy grapes like Cinsaut and Carignan, so it is great with highly flavoured food.

Fitou (*fee-too*)	AC	Mxd	F

Over the last ten years this has become a favourite in Britain, and deservedly so. However, and luckily for Bootful-minded people, it still remains rela-tively cheap.

Fitou vineyards form two enclaves in the Corbières district of Languedoc-Roussillon. The wines produced are rich, lightly spicy – the spice comes from the southern Carignan and Grenache grapes – and great all rounders.

Recommended producers include Madame Parmentier (probably the best-known), but most Fitou is of very high quality.

Fleurie (*fleur-ee*)　　　　AC　　Gam　　FF

One of the most famous of the ten Beaujolais villages (known as 'Crus'), and hence often one of the most pricey. Fleurie is known throughout the region as the queen of Beaujolais. The wines have a certain elegance and charm, with lots of floral aromas and flavours. However, while the quality is fairly consistent, better value can often be had from other Beaujolais Crus such as Chénas or Chiroubles (*see* pages 131–33).

Recommended producers include Chanut, Duboeuf, Eventail de Producteurs, Ferraud, Fessy, Loron, Mommessin and Sarrau.

Fronsac (*fronn-sack*)　　　AC　　Mer/CF　　FF

Fronsac lies just outside St-Emilion, and produces wines of a similar style. It is not yet as well-known as its more famous neighbour, but some of the area's leading producers think it deserves to be.

The wines are soft and chocolatey, with blackcurrant flavours when young. Some winemakers use new oak for ageing, adding a touch of vanilla to the flavour, but most do not.

Recommended producers include Châteaux Dalem, de la Dauphine, La Rivière, Clos du Roy and Villars.

Gard (*gar*)　　　　　　VDP　　Mxd　　F

Gard is the *département* (the French equivalent of an English county) situated between the Ardèche and the Mediterranean, where vineyards flourish around the town of Nîmes. It is a large area and the red wines it produces are reliable, cheap and great Bootful material. They are made from the classic southern blend of Carignan, Grenache, Cinsaut and Syrah grapes, with a dash of Merlot and Cabernet Sauvignon added to give smoothness and good currant fruit.

Gevrey-Chambertin   AC   PN   FFF
(*sjev-ree shom-bare-tan*)

One of the most famous of all red burgundies, Gevrey-Chambertin can be over-priced and over-produced. This is a pity because wine from serious growers is amongst the best in the world. The straight village wine (Gevrey) is hardly ever worth buying, but look out for the Grand Crus with names ending in '-Chambertin' (*see* the Chambertin entry, page 130) which can be mind-blowing.

Gigondas   AC   Mxd   FF
(*sjee-gonn-dass*)

This is one of the best appellations in the southern Rhône, so if you like spicy, rich reds, give its wine a place in your Bootful.

The vineyards surround the village of the same name, which is derived from the Latin meaning 'merry city': one taste of this gloriously rich, purple-black wine with its plummy, spicy character will show you just how apt this is.

Gigondas is made predominantly from Grenache blended with other local grapes. Whilst most is drunk young, a good one will age successfully for up to ten years.

Recommended producers include Chapoutier, Paul Jaboulet Aîné, the *cave coopérative*, and domaine-bottled wines.

Givry (*sjee-vree*)   AC   PN   FF

Although also a red burgundy, don't confuse Givry with Gevrey (as in Gevrey-Chambertin, *see* the preceding page) – the wines are completely different. Gevrey-Chambertin comes from the Côte d'Or, and Givry is produced in the Mercurey region near Chalon-sur-Saône.

Givry's wines are soft, easy-drinking, with lots of solid raspberry overtones. They can be good Bootful wines as they are often priced towards the cheaper end of the medium ('FF') bracket.

Recommended producers include Chofflet, Joblot and Baron Thénard.

Graves (*grahv*)   AC   Mer/CF   FF–FFF

This area lies to the south of the city of Bordeaux, and produces a large number of red (and white) wines. The most famous is Château Haut-Brion, whose vineyards are actually in the suburbs of Bordeaux. At their best, Graves are silky-smooth wines, with exotic aromas and flavours. They can be drunk younger than their cousins from the Médoc, as, instead of Cabernet Sauvignon, the Merlot grape variety is normally the dominant one in the blend.

The best-known Graves are not really Bootful wines (in fact, the better known Graves are now entitled to the higher appellation of Pessac-Léognan, *see* pages 154–55), but sometimes lesser châteaux' can be. Before buying any in quantity, try a bottle.

Recommended producers, all at the 'FF' price level, include Châteaux Cabannieux, Chicane, La Grave, Rahoul and Roquetaillade La Grange.

Hautes-Côtes de Beaune   AC   PN   F–FF
(*oat-coat der bone*)

Situated on the hills which spread to the west of the Côte de Beaune, overlooking the more famous vineyards. This large area makes wines less common than one might expect. At their best they are soft, with delicious raspberry Pinot Noir flavours.

Those recommended include Guillemard-Dupont, who also makes an interesting white Pinot Beurot.

Hautes-Côtes de Nuits   AC   PN   F–FF
(*oat-coat der nwee*)

This is a smaller area than the Hautes-Côtes de Beaune, but its situation is similar as it is found up in the hills west of Nuits-St-Georges.

The quality is possibly better than that of the Côte de Beaune's equivalent, and the best wines have delicious, quite intense, raspberry/oaky flavours.

Recommended producers include Dufouleur, Hudelot, Jayer-Gilles and Thévenot-Le Brun.

Hérault (*air-row*)   VDP   Mxd   F

Hérault is an area of the Languedoc-Roussillon region in the south of France stretching along the

GRAPE VARIETIES FOR MEDIUM-BODIED RED WINES		CS/Mer	Cabernet Sauvignon /Merlot blend
CS	Cabernet Sauvignon	**PRICE CODE**	
CF	Cabernet Franc	F	Cheap: less than 20 francs a bottle.
Gam	Gamay		
Mer	Merlot	FF	Medium: 20–70 francs a bottle.
PN	Pinot Noir		
Syr	Syrah	FFF	Expensive: more than 70 francs a bottle.
Mxd	Mixed		

Mediterranean coast from Montpellier in the east to Minervois in the west. It covers many zones, all entitled to use their own *vin de pays* name.

Hérault wines are of consistent quality and its reds are smooth with good fruit. They are made from the popular, widely planted southern French grapes: Carignan, Grenache, Cinsaut and Syrah, with small amounts of Cabernet Sauvignon and Merlot sometimes added too. There are many Bootful bargains to be had from this good value appellation.

Juliénas   AC   Gam   FF
(*sjoo-lee-ay-nass*)

A value for money Beaujolais Cru, made, like its neighbours, from the hugely drinkable Gamay grape. This is one of the more full-bodied wines of Beaujolais, with powerful fruit flavour and enough tannin to ensure the wine can last well. Juliénas lies to the north of Moulin-à-Vent, and is almost as full-bodied as the latter (*see* page 153). But, possibly because its name is more difficult to pronounce, it remains a much better buy for the Bootful.

Recommended producers include Chanut, Duboeuf, Eventail de Producteurs, Ferraud, Fessy, Loron, Mommessin and Sarrau.

Lalande de Pomerol   AC   Mer/CF   FF
(*la-land der pomm-air-oll*)

Potentially an area of great Bootful treasures in the Bordeaux region. Lalande de Pomerol lies to the north of Pomerol itself, and the wines are of much the same style (*see* pages 155–56). Although they will never achieve the heights of the top Pomerols, they are nevertheless, lush, rich and very attractive.

They are based on the Merlot grape and so can be drunk relatively young, from three years after the vintage onwards.

Recommended producers include Châteaux des Annereaux, Bel-Air, Siaurac and Tournefeuille.

Listrac (*lee-strack*) AC CS/Mer FF

Listrac is one of only six regions in the famous Médoc (in Bordeaux) to be allowed its own appellation. Sadly, it almost never lives up to what should be its potential. If it is claret you are after, you can do much better buying elsewhere.

Lot (*lott*) VDP Mxd F–FF

This region lies to the east of the river Dordogne and produces decent quality reds which, as the name suggests, are well worth buying for the Bootful. Classic Bordeaux grapes like Cabernet Sauvignon and Merlot are blended with local grapes to make these mid-weight fruity wines, best enjoyed young.

Lussac St-Emilion AC Mer/CF FF
(*loose-ack sant-emm-ee-lee-onn*)

One of the satellite appellations outside St-Emilion. Provided the price is right you can sometimes find some bargain Bootful wines from this one. They are much softer than Bordeaux from the Médoc and they should be drunk young. Don't buy any in quantity without tasting first – the quality is very variable.

Recommended producers include Châteaux Cap de Merle, du Courlat, de Lussac and Milon.

Mâcon (*mack-on*) AC Gam/PN F–FF

These reds can be great value for money, provided they are cheap. Mâcon Rouge is made in a predominantly white wine region, and the reds tend to come a poor second. They are a blend of Gamay and Pinot Noir, and are something of an acquired taste with their earthy, fairly acidic flavour and tangy underlying raspberry fruit. Make sure you taste before you buy.

Recommended producers include Chanut, Duboeuf, Eventail de Producteurs, Ferraud, Fessy, Loron, Mommessin and Sarrau.

Mercurey (*mare-cure-ee*) AC PN FF

To the south of the famous Côte d'Or, on the way to Mâcon and Beaujolais, the wines of this region are all too often overlooked. This is great news for the Bootful bargain hunter as its prices have therefore not yet hit the heady heights reached by many other red burgundies.

Mercurey wines are full of fruit, yet can be both elegant and subtle, the best having really good Pinot Noir flavour.

Those with 'Premier Cru' on the label come from named vineyards, they are more concentrated and, of course, more expensive (but normally worth it).

Recommended producers include Michel Juillot, de Launay and Domaine Saier.

Montagne St-Emilion AC Mer/CF F–FF
(*monn-tanya sant-emm-ee-lee-onn*)

This is a large area to the north of St-Emilion, in Bordeaux – it is one of St-Emilion's satellite appellations. Montagne St-Emilion can produce reasonable Bootful wines. Unfortunately though, having St-Emilion in its name could be seen to have gone to its head as all too many of them are overpriced and under quality. You might be lucky enough to find one worth buying, but tread carefully.

Recommended producers include Châteaux Calon, Grand-Baril, des Tours and Vieux Château St-André (this last is owned by the oenologist of Château Pétrus – Jean-Pierre Moueix).

Morey-St-Denis	AC	PN	FFF
(*mo-ree san den-ee*)			

One of the very top red burgundies from the Côte de Nuits region. When it's at its best it has wonderfully sumptuous, classic raspberry Pinot Noir flavours.

If you can find any at all in the 'FF' price range, you are doing well. Sadly, this is not really a Bootful wine.

Morgon (*more-gone*)	AC	Gam	FF

The phonetic spelling of this Beaujolais Cru really sums it up – as soon as a glass is put in front of you, it's gone, and you want more!

The wines are relatively full-bodied (compared to many from Beaujolais) and have a seductive, cherry-like flavour. And while they can be enjoyable to drink when quite young, they will mature well too. They are certainly a sound investment for your Bootful.

Recommended producers include Chanut, Duboeuf, Eventail de Producteurs, Ferraud, Fessy, Loron, Mommessin and Sarrau.

Moulin à Vent	AC	Gam	FF
(*moo-lann a vonn*)			

This wine is aptly known as 'the king of Beaujolais' – it is the most full-bodied and longest-lasting of all the Beaujolais Crus.

While it still has the unmistakable aroma of the fruity, gulpable Gamay on the palate, its structure is much tougher and denser than its neighbours', with much more tannin than most beaujolais. These are wines which taste better after five to ten years in the bottle – Bootful wine to lay down and forget about for a few years.

Recommended producers include Chanut, Duboeuf, Eventail de Producteurs, Ferraud, Fessy, Loron, Mommessin and Sarrau.

Nuits-St-Georges	AC	PN	FF–FFF
(*nwee sann-sjor-jer*)			

Because this burgundy is so well-known and normally over-priced, it is not really Bootful material. Occasionally you might come across a Nuits-St-Georges which is worth the money, but you'll really have to search the shelves. When it is good it will be quite chunky (for burgundy) with full, plummy fruit.

Recommended growers include Boisset, Faiveley, Jayer, Moillard, Rion and Vienot.

Oc	VDP	Mxd	F
(*'ock', but normally seen as d'Oc, pronounced 'dock'*)			

Vins de Pays d'Oc can come from anywhere in the large Languedoc-Roussillon region in the south of France.

Ten years ago they were mostly stewed, jammy and unpleasant. Today, improved vinification techniques have changed all that, and wines from this *vin de pays* now reflect the care taken to make them: they are full of tasty, easy-drinking, ripe, southern fruit character and are good value for money too – ideal fillers for the Bootful.

A wide range of grapes can be used which include Cabernet Sauvignon, Cabernet Franc, Carignan, Grenache, Merlot, Syrah and Mourvèdre. Increasingly, though, producers are making single varietal wines, the grape variety used being named on the label.

Pécharmant   AC   Mer/CF   F–FF
(*pay-shar-monn*)

This relatively unknown region is in the centre of the Bergerac appellation (*see* page 125) near Bordeaux. It is situated in bull's eye position, and if you hit it, you'll get a good score for your Bootful as the wines really are top quality. They taste like mini clarets and yet cost just a fraction of their price.

Recommended producers include Château Corbiac, Domaine du Haut Pécharmant and Château La Renaudie.

Pessac-Léognan   AC   CS/Mer   FF–FFF
(*pess-ack lay-oh-nyonn*)

This is a relatively new Bordeaux appellation which incorporates some of the oldest names of the Graves region, classifying them at a higher level than just straight Graves (*see* page 147).

The wines are silky-smooth and can be incredibly stylish and complex. The epitome of Pessac-Léognan is Château Haut-Brion, one of the greatest wines of Bordeaux. Sadly, though, Pessac-Léognan is not really Bootful material as the prices are normally in the 'FFF' price range.

Recommended producers whose wines might sometimes fall into the 'FF' category include Châteaux Bouscaut, Carbonnieux, de Fieuzal, de France, La Louvière, Malartic-Lagravière, and Smith-Haut-Lafitte.

Pomerol (*pomm-er-oll*) AC Mer/CF FFF

One of the smallest of the Bordeaux vineyard areas, yet also one of the most famous. Pomerol is the home of Château Pétrus, which produces the world's most expensive wine, never selling for less than £100 a bottle – and that's for a very ordinary vintage. Pomerol is situated next to St-Emilion (*see* page 159), and the most important grape there is Merlot, producing rich, chocolatey wines that can be enjoyed young.

Sadly, most Pomerols are too expensive for Bootful buyers, and you would be better advised to look for wines from Lalande de Pomerol – a neighbouring appellation whose reds are often extremely good value (*see* pages 149–50).

GRAPE VARIETIES FOR MEDIUM-BODIED RED WINES		CS/Mer	Cabernet Sauvignon /Merlot blend
CS	Cabernet Sauvignon	**PRICE CODE**	
CF	Cabernet Franc	F	Cheap: less than 20 francs a bottle.
Gam	Gamay		
Mer	Merlot	FF	Medium: 20–70 francs a bottle.
PN	Pinot Noir		
Syr	Syrah	FFF	Expensive: more than 70 francs a bottle.
Mxd	Mixed		

When buying this one though, one of the safest names to look for on a label is Jean-Pierre Moueix, who also makes Château Pétrus.

Recommended wines sometimes in the 'FF' price range include Châteaux Le Bon Pasteur, Bourgneuf-Vayron, Clinet, Clos du Clocher, La Croix, Mazeyres, Moulinet, Nenin, Plince, La Pointe, Rouget, de Sales, du Tailhas and Taillefer.

Pommard (*pomm-arr*) AC PN FFF

One of the most famous Côte de Beaune villages, producing velvety, sumptuous, raspberry-flavoured wines on a good day. On a bad day, forget it, as they can be a rip-off. These are not really Bootful material, as the best growers produce so little that their wines are never sold cheaply.

Recommended growers whose wines occasionally fall into the 'FF' price range include Boillot, Leflaive, Marchard de Gramont, Montille, Mussy, Parent and Pothier-Rieusset.

Premières Côtes de Blaye AC Mer/CF F–FF
(*premm-ee-air coat der bly*)

All claret lovers should make a note of this name as this appellation, on the east bank of the Gironde estuary, facing the Médoc, produces excellent value for money clarets. They tend to be softer, more early-maturing than those of the Médoc, with lots of violet-like fruit from the Merlot grape. If you like St-Emilion wines then it is well worth trying these.

It is not just the taste that makes Premières Côtes de Blaye appealing – their price makes them serious contenders for your Bootful too.

Recommended producers include Châteaux Bourdieu, Charron, Grand Barrail, Haut-Sociondo, Peyredoulle, Segonzac and La Tonnelle.

Premières Côtes de Bordeaux   AC Mer/CF F–FF
(*premm-ee-air coat der bore-doe*)

Don't confuse this appellation's name with the Premier Cru Classés of the Médoc. The latter are Bordeaux's most famous (and expensive) reds, while these wines are much more affordable.

The Premières Côtes de Bordeaux area is large, running alongside the river Garonne (on the right bank) from north of the city of Bordeaux, right down to Sauternes in the south. Until about ten years ago the wines were eminently forgettable, but now they are some of Bordeaux's best bargains.

There are many small châteaux in the region, and your best bet is to taste some of their wines and decide for yourself which you like best.

Pyrénées-Orientales   VDP   Mxd   F
(*pee-renn-ay orr-ee-enn-tahl*)

Quality reds come from this large, Pyrenees-shaded *vin de pays* area in Languedoc-Roussillon. They are robust, with masses of blackberry-like fruit, yet are more soft than tannic on the finish. Produced to a consistently high standard, and sold at very good prices too, these are ideal Bootful wines which are great for large parties.

Régnié (*ray-nee-ay*)   AC   Gam   FF

The most recent Beaujolais village to be elevated to 'Cru' status; the Régnié appellation could be seen by cynics as an excuse for Beaujolais growers to hike up the prices of wines from the western edge of their region.

They are very light wines, even for beaujolais, and the best have lots of tasty fruit. However, it has to be said that there are much better bargains to be had from other Beaujolais regions, even at the Beaujolais-Villages level. This Cru is not yet seen widely outside the region of production.

Recommended producers include Chanut, Duboeuf, Eventail de Producteurs, Ferraud, Fessy, Loron, Mommessin and Sarrau.

Richebourg (*reesh-boorg*)   AC   PN   FFF

This is the stuff that dreams are made of. Richebourg is one of the top red burgundies from the Côte de Nuits. Only a handful of producers make it, and at its best it is mind-blowing. There's no way this is Bootful material, as a small mortgage would be needed to fill up the boot with it!

Sables du Golfe du Lion   VDP   Mxd   F
(*sah-bl dew golf dew lee-on*)

You can walk through the vineyards in this region and feel sand between your toes; the vines are planted on the Mediterranean-skirting sand dunes of the Camargue, the river Rhône's great estuary.

Sables du Golfe du Lion reds are fruity with a spicy element, and taste good both on holiday and when you get back home! They are sound, inexpensive, but good quality Bootful material.

Wine production is dominated by the quality conscious Domaines Viticoles des Salins du Midi – better known by its brand name, Listel.

St-Amour (*sant-amm-oor*)   AC   Gam   FF

It is easy to fall in love with this evocatively named Beaujolais Cru wine, as it is the most delicate of the ten Crus'. Situated the furthest north of all of them, St-Amour shows that the Gamay grape can be more than just gulpable, it can be elegant too.

Its attractive name has tended to elevate its price a little but nevertheless, it is a sound Bootful candidate for anyone who is romantically minded.

Recommended producers include Chanut, Duboeuf, Eventail de Producteurs, Ferraud, Fessy, Loron, Mommessin and Sarrau.

St-Emilion   AC   Mer/CF   FF–FFF
(*sant emm-ee-lee-onn*)

This well-known name is an area outside the town of Libourne, on the right bank of the Dordogne river. The wine produced is claret, although, because the Merlot grape is the predominant one (rather than the other traditional Bordeaux grape, Cabernet Sauvignon, which needs more time to mellow), most of the wines can be drunk relatively young and don't have to be kept for years until they are ready.

However, despite the relatively high price of these wines, not every bottle labelled as St-Emilion is worth buying. There are probably more poor quality wines from this area than most others, so it is essential you sample some before buying any in quantity.

There are hundreds of châteaux in St-Emilion, and there is not the space to list them all here. But recommended producers whose wines sometimes fall into the 'FF' price range include Châteaux

Cadet-Piola, Dassault, La Dominique, Fombrauge, Pavie-Decesse, La Serre, Troplong-Mondot and Yon-Figeac.

St-Julien AC CS/Mer FF–FFF
(*sann-sjew-lee-ann*)

This is one of the areas which produces classic red Bordeaux. It is small, covering just one gravel bank on the left of Bordeaux's Gironde estuary, and the area of production can never be extended, so there will always be only a limited supply.

The best wines can last for decades, and have wonderful flavours of concentrated ripe blackcurrants, mixed with vanilla from the oak barrels in which they are aged before bottling.

Recommended producers whose wines sometimes fall into the 'FF' price bracket include Châteaux Les Fiefs-de-Lagrange, du Glana, Lalande-Borie, Langoa-Barton, and Terrey-Gros-Caillou.

Sancerre (*sonn-serr*) AC PN FF

Last century, most of the production of this hilltop town in the Loire Valley was of red wine, until the vines were destroyed by the vine-eating louse, Phylloxera. Fortunately, although the replanting which followed was mostly with white grape vine varieties (they grow much faster than black grape vines), some Pinot Noir was re-established too.

Red Sancerre is delicious, like a rather more earthy version of red burgundy. It is a very refreshing wine and is particularly attractive when drunk chilled. A great one for your Bootful.

Recommended producers include Dezat, Laporte, Vacheron and Vatan.

Santenay (*sonn-ten-ay*)   AC   PN   FF

Santenay is the most southerly area of the Côte d'Or, and its wines can be great value. The best will have masses of ripe, raspberry fruit with some classic, burgundy-like, farmyardy smells. Quality is very varied, so taste carefully before buying.

Recommended producers include Bouzereau, Girardin, Morey and Pousse d'Or.

Saumur (*so-mure*)   AC   CF   FF

When you are bored with Cabernet Sauvignon or conventional reds in general, a Saumur Rouge can provide a welcome change. It is a refreshing, juicy wine from vineyards surrounding the attractive château town of the same name. This is Cabernet Franc at its best: a fresh, grassy aroma, masses of tangy red fruit flavours on the palate, and zippy acidity on the finish. Without a doubt it is a Bootful wine, and one to be enjoyed chilled.

Saumur-Champigny   AC   CF   FF
(*so-mure shom-peen-yee*)

These wines have all the character traits of Saumur, and more. The produce of the village of Champigny,

GRAPE VARIETIES FOR MEDIUM-BODIED RED WINES		CS/Mer	Cabernet Sauvignon /Merlot blend
CS	Cabernet Sauvignon	**PRICE CODE**	
CF	Cabernet Franc	F	Cheap: less than 20 francs a bottle.
Gam	Gamay		
Mer	Merlot	FF	Medium: 20–70 francs a bottle.
PN	Pinot Noir		
Syr	Syrah	FFF	Expensive: more than 70 francs a bottle.
Mxd	Mixed		

they are more intense, with more depth of fruit, as well as more bitter tannin. Because of this they can age well, and, after five years or so, develop much greater depth of flavour. This is one of my favourites, and a good Bootful wine for special lunches and suppers.

Recommended producers include Domaine Filliatreau and Alain Sanzay.

Savigny-lès-Beaune AC PN FF
(*sav-een-yee lay bone*)

Right up in the north of the Côte de Beaune, Savigny produces wonderful, fairly light, but very tasty wines from Pinot Noir grapes. The best are heavily scented, with ripe, raspberry flavours. They can be enjoyed young, but will also keep for up to 15 years.

Recommended growers include Girard-Vollot and Bize.

Vacqueyras AC Mxd FF
(*vack-ay-rass*)

A southern Rhône beauty, just ripe for the Bootful. Vacqueyras is situated between Gigondas and Beaumes-de-Venise (famous for its alcoholic sweet white – *see* page 108) and produces stunning, value for money reds. On the full side of medium-bodied, these are wines with a good purple/black colour when young, and masses of plummy fruit aromas and ripe spiciness, with moderate tannin on the palate. Because of this you can drink them relatively soon after their vintage, or you can keep them for a few years.

Recommended producers include Paul Jaboulet

Aîné, Château de Montmirail, Cave du Troubour and the *cave coopérative*.

Vallée du Paradis   VDP   Mxd   F
(*vall-ay dew parr-add-ees*)

An apt name indeed for this typical Bootful wine. You could easily feel as if you were in paradise when you taste it and then realise how cheap it is.

Situated south of Narbonne, this *vin de pays* forms part of the quality-producing region of the Languedoc-Roussillon. Classic southern grapes (Carignan, Grenache, Syrah and Cinsaut) get a bit of extra help from smaller percentages of Cabernet Sauvignon and Merlot in this wine. The result is an ideal claret substitute. It has lots of ripe berry fruit on the aroma and palate, and enough tannin to balance it without making it bitter. A good food wine.

Recommended producers include Val d'Orbieu.

Var (*var*)   VDP   Mxd   F

A huge *vin de pays* area in the south of France, stretching right down to Toulon on the coast.

Its red wines are well made and cheap – good for parties. They are made from a blend of spicy southern grapes mixed with the blackcurrant-flavoured Cabernet Sauvignon. On the heavy side of medium-bodied they have lots of good, firm, peppery fruit and enough tannin on the finish. Make sure your Bootful includes some Var-iety!

Vaucluse (*voh-clues*)   VDP   Mxd   F

This wine is produced in vineyards to the east of Orange and Avignon in the Rhône Valley. It is similar in style to Côtes du Rhône (*see* pages 141–42), but often has more depth and underlying spicy fruit. Because this is a humble *vin de pays* region, rather than an *appellation contrôlee*, prices are very reasonable.

Volnay (*voll-nay*)   AC   PN   FF–FFF

From burgundy's Côte de Beaune, this wine can be either fabulously soft and structured, or otherwise dull and boring. At its best it will be silky smooth with great complexity and the ability to mature well for many years. However, because of its price it will never be Bootful material, and buying in quantity without having tasted first is potentially disastrous.

Recommended producers whose wines occasionally fall into the 'FF' price bracket include Delagrange, Lafarge, Leflaive and Pousse d'Or.

Vosne-Romanée   AC   PN   FFF
(*vone-rome-ann-ay*)

One of the ultimate wines from Burgundy's Côte de Nuits, made from the Pinot Noir grape. At its best it is incredibly complex, with intense raspberry flavours, and is one of the greatest wines in the world. At its worst it is desperately boring and very over-priced.

The dreary ones are not nearly cheap enough, and the best will never have any reason to drop their price. Sadly, Vosne-Romanée is unlikely ever to be a suitable wine for your Bootful.

CHAPTER 13

FULL-BODIED REDS

Rich, robust and red sum up these delicious wines. They are shown to their best advantage with fully flavoured food and are also great to have in store for cold rainy days when you really need a drop of something tasty to warm you up – they have excellent potential for the Bootful. Many actually improve with keeping too, so it is a good idea to tuck some away and forget about them for a few years.

Full-bodied red wines are not only full in flavour, they are full in colour too. Many are inky, purple/black rather than the normal, paler red shades of the medium-bodied wines. They're also full in tannin: the bitter, mouth-puckering substance from the grape skins which helps give wines their body and structure (you'll recognise this as it is found in tea and coffee too). Tannin is an important part of these wines, though sometimes they need to mature for a number of years for it to soften out. France's classic full-bodied reds from Bordeaux and the northern Rhône, for example, both need to be kept for decades before they are ready to drink.

Some of these robust reds have been aged in oak barrels, which add more tannin to the wine, as well as enhancing it with rich, vanilla-like characteristics.

Full-bodied reds are not for the faint hearted and are unlikely to appeal if you do not normally drink red wine. For those of us who do, however, they are delicious, and sum up all that is best about it.

They cry out for equally strongly flavoured foods. Serve them with full-bodied casseroles and stews, spicy chilli dishes or curries (drink them chilled with these), or Provençale inspired dishes laced with garlic and herbs. They are ideal with hung game like venison and pheasant, or roast red meats, especially those served with rich, creamy or peppery sauces. They are also a good foil to dishes cooked with a reduced red wine base, which can be so powerful they knock medium reds for six.

Strong cheddar, soft strong cheeses like runny brie, blue cheese or goats' cheese: all these too have flavours which balance well with robust reds'.

And some richer, slighter sweeter reds (from the south of France) are strangely successful with richly flavoured desserts, even chocolate or coffee based ones which tend to smother many a lesser wine.

Full-bodied reds in the 'F' price category are stunning value and should always have a place in your Bootful. However, as a general rule, the more you pay for one in France, the less good value it is, and the cheaper (relatively) it will be in Britain.

The Wines

KEY TO GRAPE VARIETY ABBREVIATIONS
   Syr   Syrah
   CS/Mer   Cabernet Sauvignon/Merlot blend
   Mxd   Mixed

Bandol (*ban-doll*)	AC	Mxd	FF

Just one whiff of the sun-baked, spicy grapes in this southern French red wine conjures up the image of a delicious Provençale feast in the sunshine. They are so loaded with ripe fruit that to smell them is almost enough – except that one can't resist drinking them too.

Produced in spectacular vineyards, beside huge cliffs which overlook the Mediterranean, Bandol grapes make wines with extremely concentrated fruitiness. They are black and inky in colour and have lots of spicy, plummy fruit flavour with quite a lot of bitter tannin when young. Bandol wines can last for ages so it is definitely worth laying down a few bottles or cases and forgetting about them for five to ten years before sampling.

Recommended producers include Paul and Pierre Bunan (especially their Mas de la Rouvière) and Domaine Tempier.

Cahors (*ka-oar*)   AC   Mxd   F–FF

Deep purple Cahors is always a good bet if you are into full-bodied reds. Produced around the town of the same name in the Lot *département*, to the east-southeast of Bordeaux, these are like monster versions of the famous Bordeaux claret.

The main grape used is Malbec, with spicy, plummy, liquorice and currant flavours and masses of full-bodied tannin; Merlot and Tannat are used too. Definitely good for body building Bootfuls!

Châteauneuf-du-Pape   AC   Mxd   FF–FFF
(*shat-oh-neuf dew pap*)

This wine comes with a red-hot holy recommend-ation, as it is reputed to have been the favourite tipple of the 14th-century Avignon pope, John XXII. He built a castle close to these vineyards, hence the name – translated it means 'the pope's new castle'.

One of the best wines produced in the southern Rhône, Châteauneuf-du-Pape is made from a blend of 13 permitted grape varieties, including the northern Rhône's Syrah, as well as Grenache, Mourvèdre, Cinsaut and Terret Noir. All are grown on famous soil: it is made up of large pebbles, so special, according to growers, that they are actually responsible for Châteauneuf's most distinctive qualities.

This spicy wine has a slightly gamey flavour and lots of full-bodied fruit, without too much mouth-puckering tannin. This means that while it can mature well, it is not too bitter to drink young.

Recommended producers include Château de Beaucastel, Chante Cigale, Château Rayas and Domaine du Vieux Télégraphe.

Cité de Carcassonne VDP Mxd F
(*sit-ay der car-cass-on*)

Carcassonne is an attractive historic walled hilltop town, producing equally attractive red wines. And they are cheap too so are good Bootful material!

The *vin de pays* area covers eleven villages in the Aude region, and its wines are made from a mixture of grapes including Carignan, Syrah, Merlot, Cinsaut and Cabernet Sauvignon.

They combine hefty red and black berry fruit flavours, with lots of spicy, rustic, plummy fruit. And while full-bodied, they are easy to drink too, and go well with fairly robust, obvious flavours like barbecued or very herby or garlicky food.

Corbières (*kor-bee-air*) AC Mxd F–FF

This full-bodied red is produced south of Carcassonne and is a typically southern, spicy wine. Made mainly from Carignan and Grenache, it varies in style from medium through to heavy weight. As a general rule, the cheaper ones are in the medium category, while the more expensive are full-bodied, with added nuances of vanilla gained during their maturation period in oak barrels.

Corbières used to be very popular amongst British wine-drinkers who knew France, and is now finding new fans amongst those who have never been to the country. Its increasingly well-known name is a reflection of its character: generally very reliable and good value – great news for the Bootful.

Cornas (*kor-nass*) AC Syr FF–FFF

One of the best heavyweight reds from the northern Rhône, Cornas is better value than its more famous neighbour, Hermitage. It is a blockbuster that, tasted young, can be so bitter you may think it undrinkable. But after five or ten years the tannin will have softened out, allowing the fruit of the Syrah grape to emerge: an intense aroma of spicy blackcurrants mixed with raspberries, lots of vanilla, and smokey spice on the palate is revealed.

Buy a few bottles and forget about them for a few years. Then try a bottle to see how the wine is tasting, remembering to drink it with very powerfully flavoured food like game.

Recommended producers include Auguste Clape, Paul Jaboulet Aîné and Alain Voge.

Côte Rôtie (*coat roat-ee*) AC Syr FF–FFF

The name of this wine translates as 'roasted slope' and is a good description both of the rich, roasted wine and the appellation's location. The vines are grown on the steep, terraced vineyards at the far north of the Rhône Valley, where the powerfully spicy black grape Syrah is king. Unusually for a red wine of this style and class, it includes a small proportion of white grapes (up to 15%).

The best Côte Rôtie is intensely strong, yet also elegant, with a roasted coffee and spice aroma and lots of thick, rich fruit and bitter tannin. These are wines which can taste revolting when young, but last for years – after five to 20 the tannin will have softened out and they will be quite sensational.

Recommended: Bernard Burgaud, Champet, Guigal, Paul Jaboulet Aîné, Jasmin, and Vidal Fleury.

Coteaux d'Aix en Provence   AC   Mxd   F–FF
(*cot-oh dakes on prov-onse*)

In this southern region quality wines are produced that are both pleasant for drinking now and will also last for a few years. They are weighty, yet classy, with an aroma that reminds me of blackcurrant tart with cream and a hint of vanilla essence.

Grapes used include Grenache, Carignan and Syrah, plus a fair proportion of the classic claret grape, Cabernet Sauvignon – hence the strong blackcurrant flavours in some of the wines. They are certainly good Bootful material.

Recommended producers include Châteaux de Fonscolombe and Vignelaure.

Côtes de Provence   AC   Mxd   F–FF
(*coat der prov-onse*)

This region produces thousands of litres of very quaffable rosé, normally in skittle-shaped bottles. Its red wines are well worth trying too. They are good quality and made in many different styles, some which can be laid down and kept, and others which can be fun, easy-drinking, great party reds. A number are good value, but you need to look at prices carefully as this is not a general rule.

Similar grapes are used as in the neighbouring appellation, Coteaux d'Aix-en-Provence (*see opposite*); here they seem to lend an added spicy, plummy, liquorice aroma and flavour.

Recommended producers include Les Maitres Vignerons de la Presqu'ile de St-Tropez, but there are many others worth looking for. The quality overall is consistently high.

Côtes du Roussillon   AC   Mxd   F–FF
(*coat dew roose-ee-on*)

Dismissed, until a few years ago, as rough southern red, this region of the Midi is today producing some really good quality wines.

They are made mainly from Carignan, with some Mourvèdre and Syrah added: purple/black in colour, with an intense aroma of ripe blackberries, lots of spicy fruit, and often hints of vanilla on the finish. Quality is fairly consistent too throughout the region. All in all, excellent Bootful wines.

Côtes du Roussillon-Villages come from 25 specific villages and are even more concentrated. But this one extra word does add to their price – a difference it is not always worth paying.

GRAPE VARIETIES FOR FULL-BODIED RED WINES		PRICE CODE	
Syr	Syrah	F	Cheap: less than 20 francs a bottle.
CS/Mer	Cabernet Sauvignon/ Merlot blend	FF	Medium: 20–70 francs a bottle.
Mxd	Mixed	FFF	Expensive: more than 70 francs a bottle.

Haut-Médoc   AC   CS/Mer   FF–FFF
(*oh med-ock*)

This is a large region of Bordeaux, including in its boundaries the famous appellations of St-Estèphe, Pauillac, St-Julien, Margaux, Listrac and Moulis. However, wines labelled with the words Haut-Médoc will generally be from outside these areas.

The appellation Médoc (on its own) covers an even more extensive region, although similarly, it is a 'catch all', and wines labelled as such do not include the famous châteaux.

Because neither Haut-Médoc nor Médoc carry the prestige of the better known Bordeaux appellations, some good Bootful wines can be found from properties classified at this level.

The best Haut-Médocs will have the typical delicious blackcurranty flavour of good Bordeaux, and will be full-bodied with a noticeable amount of tannin when young (five years old or younger). They are made mostly from Cabernet Sauvignon grapes, normally blended with Merlot and Cabernet Franc, as is traditional in Bordeaux.

Médoc wines are made from the same blends; they will be slightly less tannic and are often cheaper.

Recommended producers from the Médoc and Haut-Médoc include Châteaux Beaumont, Brillette, Cantemerle, La Cardonne, Castéra, Cissac, Hanteillan, La Lagune, Lanessan, Loudenne, Les Ormes-Sorbet, Plagnac, Potensac, Sociando-Mallet, La Tour-de-By, Tour-du-Haut-Moulin and Villegorge.

Hermitage (*air-mee-tarj*)   AC   Syr   FF–FFF

The most famous wine produced in the northern Rhône, made from vines grown on steep, terraced vineyards, as impressive as the wine itself.

The sun ripens and roasts the majestic, spicy Syrah grapes until they produce a gloriously rich, purple black wine with an intense aroma of spices and berries, offset by powerful, bitter tannins. These wines will last for years (easily 20) and are for those who really enjoy full-bodied reds with an extra dimension. It's worth investing in a few bottles for special occasions.

Recommended producers include Chapoutier, Chave, Guigal, Paul Jaboulet Aîné and Sorrel.

Ile de Beauté　　　　　VDP　　　Mxd　　　F–FF
(*eel der boat-ay*)

These *vins de pays* come from the sunbaked French island of Corsica, which lies to the south of Nice and Monaco in the Mediterranean. They are produced from a variety of grapes, including Cabernet Sauvignon, Cinsaut and Grenache, as well as more unusual varieties like Aleatico and Barbarossa. They are full-bodied, with lots of peppery flavour and fruit, and without too much bitter tannin on the finish. They can be a good Bootful bargain, but should really be sampled before you buy, as quality does vary a lot.

Lirac (*lear-rack*)　　　　AC　　　Mxd　　　F

Lirac is a southern Rhône region better known for its dry rosés than its red wines, although the latter are delicious. They are well-rounded, fairly full-bodied and quite rustic in character, with soft, earthy fruit and a slightly cherry-stone flavour. Made from the classic mixture of southern Rhône grapes including Grenache, Cinsaut, Mourvèdre and Syrah, these reds complement tasty, highly spiced or barbecued food.

Madiran (*mad-ee-ron*) AC Mxd F–FF

The southwest of France produces some really beefy red wines that are almost meals in themselves, and go very well with the powerful garlic- and herb-laced food of the region. This is one of the most famous, and used to be known as the 'black' wine because of its very dark colour.

Modern methods of winemaking now mean that Madiran is far less dense than it once was, but it is still one of the heaviest wines in France, normally bursting with intense blackcurrant, meaty fruit and lots of spice and bitter tannin on the finish.

Grapes used include the local Tannat, Cabernet Sauvignon and Cabernet Franc, all of which combine to make this a vigorous wine, and a great buy for the Bootful.

Margaux (*mar-go*) AC CS/Mer FF–FFF

One of France's most famous wine names, and one of the least consistent in quality terms. These wines come from the Médoc region of Bordeaux and are made from the Cabernet Sauvignon grape, normally blended with Merlot and Cabernet Franc. A top Margaux, when mature, will be a fabulous complex mixture of blackcurrant and cedarwood flavours.

The best wines are not really Bootful wines at all, as the saving on duty is minute and they can normally be bought more cheaply in Britain. In France you will pay over the odds for the name Margaux to appear on the label.

Recommended producers whose wines are

sometimes in the 'FF' bracket include Châteaux d'Angludet, d'Issan, Labégorce, Labégorce-Zédé, Marquis-de-Terme, Monbrison and Prieuré-Lichine.

Médoc (*med-ock*)   AC   CS/Mer   F–FFF

See Haut-Médoc (page 172).

Minervois (*min-air-vwar*)   AC   Mxd   F–FF

Easy-drinking, powerful, spicy reds from an area to the northwest of Narbonne in the south of France. Minervois all have a characteristic earthy, slightly rustic edge to them, with masses of fruit and some bitter tannin. The main grape in their blend is Carignan, which gives them their distinctive aroma of spicy currants.

A good value wine which can often be bought incredibly cheaply for the Bootful.

Mont Bouquet   VDP   Mxd   F
(*mon-boo-kay*)

This is an up and coming *vin de pays* region, producing lots of easy-drinking, full-bodied, yet not too tannic reds. Grenache, Carignan and Cinsaut are blended with Cabernet Sauvignon and Syrah to give them extra colour and a spicy flavour. Bargain Bootful material.

Moulis (*moo-lees*)   AC   CS/Mer   FF–FFF

One of the six Médoc appellations, and probably the best value. When young, these Bordeaux wines are tough and tannic; they need time to soften, to reveal their wonderfully rich, balanced, blackcurrant and vanilla flavours. The best known is from Château Chasse-Spleen, and many others are well worth trying too. On the whole these are better wines than neighbouring Listrac's, and, as they fall into the same price range, they are great value.

Recommended producers: Châteaux Chasse-Spleen, Moulin-à-Vent, and anything with 'Poujeaux' in the name (eg, Gressier-Grand-Poujeaux).

Pauillac (po-yak) AC CS/Mer FF–FFF

Pauillac, in the north of Bordeaux's Médoc region, contains some of the world's most famous (and expensive) clarets; the best being the so-called 'First Growths': Châteaux Lafite-Rothschild, Mouton-Rothschild and Latour.

Pauillacs need to be kept for many years before they are ready to drink, and, apart from very average vintages like 1987 (which can be good buys) you are unlikely to find mature wines in many French shops. In addition, because the import duty is such a small part of their high cost, it is rarely worth buying them in France.

Recommended châteaux whose wines are sometimes in the 'FF' bracket include d'Armailhac, Clerc-Milon, Duhart-Milon-Rothschild, Fonbadet, Grand-Puy-Ducasse, Grand-Puy-Lacoste, Haut-Bages-Averous, Haut-Bages-Libéral, Haut-Batailley, and Pontet-Canet.

GRAPE VARIETIES FOR FULL-BODIED RED WINES		PRICE CODE	
Syr	Syrah	F	Cheap: less than 20 francs a bottle.
CS/Mer	Cabernet Sauvignon/ Merlot blend	FF	Medium: 20–70 francs a bottle.
Mxd	Mixed	FFF	Expensive: more than 70 francs a bottle.

St-Estèphe	AC	CS/Mer	FF–FFF
(*Sant est-eff*)			

The most northerly of the great Médoc vineyard areas in Bordeaux. It is quite a small region, and traditionally its wines are very tannic and somewhat lacking in appeal. However, the best châteaux have been making efforts to change this, and, whilst powerful, a good St-Estèphe will today more often have masses of enjoyable blackcurrant and vanilla flavours – though the finest still need to be kept for ten to 15 years before they are ready to drink.

The best vintages are seldom good value in France (they are too expensive) but the lesser years can be.

Recommended producers whose wines are sometimes priced in the 'FF' range: Châteaux Le Boscq, Calon-Ségur, Chambert-Marbuzet, Cos-Labory, Lafon-Rochet, Lilian-Ladoueys, Meyney, Les Ormes-de-Pez, de Pez, Phélan-Ségur and La Tour-de-Pez.

St-Joseph (*san jo-seff*)	AC	Syr	FF

Full-bodied, rich, red and very affordable are the vital statistics of this beefy northern Rhône wine. While the more famous names of this area, like Hermitage and Côte Rôtie, command higher prices, this one remains a less well known bargain.

Produced on the opposite side of the river to Crozes-Hermitage, these are made from the Syrah grape, but can be drunk much earlier than other northern Rhône greats. While the fruit and spicy plummy flavours are there, the bitter tannin is not so marked. A good saint to have in your Bootful!

Recommended producers include Boisset, Gripa, Paul Jaboulet Aîné and Paret.

CHAPTER 14

ROSÉS

These are great party wines, and the best have a refreshing appeal because they both look and taste different. Only wine snobs dismiss rosé as frivolous, but their doing so is good news for the bargain Bootful shopper as it means there is more left for us and the price is not inflated!

If you've only ever tasted Rosé d'Anjou and not liked it, don't be put off – there's a whole world of exciting fresh rosés out there just waiting to be discovered. If, on the other hand, you have only ever tasted Rosé d'Anjou and you have liked it, why not experiment with some of the others listed here?

Rosé is made from black grapes, just like red wine. But winemaking differs in that juice for rosé is left in contact with the colour-giving grape skins for a far shorter period. This 'skin contact' time can vary from just a few hours to around 12, depending on the shade required. As a result you'll see rosés of every hue, from very pale pink, to salmon, through to a much deeper, orangey red colour. No colour is incorrect, nor does shade give any indication of quality. It is simply a matter of preference.

There are some rosés which are not made by this method, however: pink champagne and sparkling rosé. These are made by blending black grape juice (from the same region) with the white grape juice base until the required colour is achieved.

Using this method it is easier for winemakers to determine the exact colour of their finished wine.

In general, the heavier, darker rosés tend to come from the south of France, areas like Ardèche, Bandol and Provence; and those from further north, the Loire Valley (Jardin de la France) for example, are much lighter both in colour and style.

Rosés are good wines to drink when you cannot decide on a red or a white; when you want some of the fruit flavours of red wines yet also want the lightness and lack of bitter tannin found in whites. They make great aperitifs when served chilled but also go well with food. Enjoy them with fish, especially salmon and trout, as well as certain shellfish like prawns, shrimps, lobsters and mussels. Slightly heavier rosés go well with regional cooking – heavily laced with herbs and olive oil – as the acidity of the wine cuts through the more oily flavours.

Meats can also be enjoyed with rosé, especially pink lamb, chicken and turkey, even rare roast beef.

Rosés are good Bootful wines, and keeping a bottle or two in the fridge is always a good idea as it can save the day when unexpected guests arrive.

The Wines

KEY TO GRAPE VARIETY ABBREVIATIONS
CF   Cabernet Franc
Mer/CS   Merlot/Cabernet Sauvignon blend
Mxd   Mixed

Ardèche (*ar-desh*)	VDP	Mxd	F

These are fullish rosés with good depth of colour. One whiff of one of these always transports me back to the sunny south of France. Soft, ripe, red berries are on the bouquet and there is clean, fresh, slightly dry fruit on the palate. The finish has a hint of spicy earthiness derived from the Carignan grape, which is blended with several other southern grapes to make this wine.

An excellent Bootful buy which goes down well as an aperitif or is full-bodied enough to cope with quite highly flavoured food.

Aude (*ode*)   VDP   Mxd   F

This rosé is produced from vineyards surrounding the walled town of Carcassonne in the heart of the Languedoc-Roussillon region. It is reasonably full-bodied, and is made from a blend of Carignan, Grenache, Cinsaut and Syrah grapes. The latter adds a certain spiciness to the aroma and flavour of this refreshingly dry but fruity wine. A good value contender for your Bootful shopping list.

Bandol (*ban-doll*)   AC   Mxd   F–FF

Bandol's vineyards have a spectacular view over the Mediterranean, to the southeast of Toulon. As a bonus, the wine is good too. Perhaps the most full-bodied of the wines in this selection of rosés. It has a ripe bouquet of fresh berries – as intense as that of many red wine aromas; and on the palate it is dry but with lots of spicy fruit flavours derived from its blend of Mourvèdre, Grenache, Cinsaut and various local grape varieties. Bandol is ideal drunk very chilled with rich, garlicky food.

Recommended producers include Domaine du Cagueloup, Domaine de la Laidière, Mas de la Rouvière, Domaine Ott, Domaine des Salettes and Domaine Tempier.

| **Bordeaux Clairet** | AC | Mer/CF | F–FF |
| *(bore-doe clare-ray)* | | | |

Don't be surprised if the word 'Clairet' looks vaguely familiar. This was the old spelling of the famous Bordeaux red wine name, claret, which at one time was more of a dark rosé than the deep red, opaque wine we know today. But as claret became more popular, this old fashioned wine which can be produced anywhere in the Bordeaux area, almost disappeared. Today it is enjoying a much-deserved renaissance, and is an unusual but worthy addition to the Bootful.

A good Clairet will be fairly deep rosé in colour, smelling of violets and blackcurrants, with full-bodied dry fruit on the palate.

Recommended producers: Châteaux Bauduc and de Sours, both British owned. Also look out for other producers from the Entre-Deux-Mers region.

| **Costières de Nîmes** | AC | Mxd | F |
| *(cost-ee-air der neem)* | | | |

Produced south of Nîmes in the Languedoc-Roussillon region, this is a medium-bodied rosé, with lots of sunny southern, rounded and easy-drinking fruit characteristics. It is very inexpensive, so load up your Bootful and drink it like the locals do, chilled and in large quantities!

| **Coteaux d'Aix en Provence** | AC | Mxd | F–FF |
| *(cot-oh dakes on prov-onse)* | | | |

These are rosé wines which are bursting with fruit, but which are also refreshingly light to drink. The Grenache grape adds a fragrant edge to them which is revealed at its best when the wine is chilled, and, once tasted, makes them hard to resist.

Include these rosés in your Bootful so that on a cold rainy day back home you can sip a glass and imagine basking in the warmth of Provence.

Ile de Beauté VDP Mxd F
(*eel der boat-ay*)

Corsica ('the beautiful island'), produces rather more rustic rosé than the rest of the south of France. It has quite an earthy, almost Italian character to it, which comes both from the local grapes blended in with the classic southern varieties like Grenache, and also the swelteringly hot climate.

Whilst the wine can be drunk on its own, it is often better served with fully flavoured, herby food.

Jardin de la France VDP Mxd F
(*sjar-dan der la fronce*)

From the Loire Valley, Vins de Pays du Jardin de la France are clean-cut, refreshing, fairly light-bodied rosés – easy to drink at any time, and very more-ish. They have plenty of mouth-watering red berry flavours from the grassy Cabernet Franc grape, and masses of fruit from the gulpable Gamay. With more roundness, but less weight than many more southern rosés, these are ideal wines for the Bootful.

Lirac (*lear-ack*) AC Mxd FF

Lirac rosé is produced southwest of Châteauneuf-du-Pape in the southern Rhône. Just like the reds of the region it is characterised by a spicy, plummy aroma and dry, yet mouth-filling fruit.

Made from Grenache and Cinsaut, with a small percentage of spicy Syrah too, it is a reliable wine, although tends to be unjustly over-shadowed by the neighbouring rosé from Tavel (*see* page 185).

Recommended producers include the Caves Coopératives de Roquemaure and des Vins de Cru Lirac.

Oc   VDP   Mxd   F
(*'ock', but normally seen as d'Oc, pronounced 'dock'*)

Vins de Pays d'Oc can come from grapes produced anywhere in the Languedoc-Roussillon region north of the Pyrenees. In line with the general trends in the south of France, the quality of this rosé has risen dramatically over the last few years. More producers have invested in new equipment to enable control of temperatures during fermentation, and, as a result, the wines have become increasingly cleaner, fresher and more fruity – a welcome change to some of the boiled, cloying rosés of the past. So they are now medium-bodied, with easy-drinking fruit. Inexpensive party wines, and great for the Bootful.

Rosé d'Anjou   AC   CF   F
(*rose-ay don-sjoo*)

The Loire Valley's answer to Piat d'Or, Rosé d'Anjou is generally medium-sweet, although those

GRAPE VARIETIES FOR ROSÉ WINES		PRICE CODE	
CF	Cabernet Franc	F	Cheap: less than 20 francs a bottle.
Mer/CS	Merlot/Cabernet Sauvignon blend	FF	Medium: 20–70 francs a bottle.
Mxd	Mixed	FFF	Expensive: more than 70 francs a bottle.

examples sold in France seem to be much drier than the sickly wine often sold in Britain.

Made mainly from the Grolleau grape, these wines are at their best drunk very young, not ageing well because of their low acidity and soft fruit character.

Because this is a well-known name you are likely to pay through the nose for it, and really, there are many better value wines to be bought for the Bootful.

Rosé Champagne   AC   Ch/PN   FF–FFF
(*sham-pain*)

See Sparkling Wines (pages 51–59).

Sables du Golfe du Lion   VDP   Mxd   F
(*sah-bl dew golf dew lee-on*)

Not only can you drink this wine on the beach, it is actually produced from vines which are grown in the sands next to the Mediterranean – in the Camargue, southeast of Montpellier. It is one of France's most elegant rosés, made from the Grenache and Cinsaut grapes, and sold as Gris de Gris, which translates literally as 'grey of grey'; the wine in fact is a very delicate, lightly tinted, salmon-pink rosé colour.

Sables du Golfe du Lion have soft fruit, yet are dry with a tangy zip to them. Load the Bootful, but always drink Gris de Gris young as the fruit tends to fade after a year or so in bottle.

This dramatic area's wine production is dominated by a quality conscious company called Domaines Viticoles des Salins du Midi who are much better known by their brand name, Listel.

| **Tavel Rosé** | AC | Mxd | FF |

(tavv-ell rose-ay)

The southern Rhône Valley's most famous rosé, produced northwest of Avignon. This wine is made from the plummy Grenache and the earthy Cinsaut grapes and is full-bodied, with a ripe, sweetish aroma, yet dry fruit on the palate. It makes a good food wine as it has an extra underlying spicy, almost peppery flavour and much more body than many other rosés. Best drunk fairly young, within five years of the vintage.

Recommended producers include the *cave coopérative* at Tavel, and most smaller producers in the area are also reliable.

| **Var** *(vahr)* | VDP | Mxd | F |

Over 50% of the rosé produced in Provence is sold under this name. Made from a blend of grapes including Grenache, Cinsaut and Syrah, the colour varies from very pale pink to a deep reddish rosé. Improved vinification techniques – such as cooled, controlled fermentation – mean that these inexpensive dry fruity wines are now consistent in quality. They are good party wines to add to the Bootful.

– CHAPTER 15 –

LIQUEURS & OTHERS

Aperitifs, Eaux de Vies and Liqueurs

If you have any space left in your Bootful you may like to take advantage of the ten litre spirit allowance.

Apart from the standard spirits like gin, vodka, whisky and cognac, French supermarkets stock a bewildering array of other, more exotic concoctions – many of which you will not find in Britain.

Calvados lovers are very well-served as all the Channel ports are fairly near Normandy, the home of this delicious spirit made from apples, and there is normally a good selection to choose from.

And if you like aniseed flavoured spirits, you'll find a wide range of different brands of pastis, all of which are subtly different. The French normally drink them mixed with water. Well-known brands include Berger, Duval, 51, Floranis, Marie-Brizard, Pernod and Ricard.

Vermouth lovers are well catered for too, with a variety of French brands available (like Byrrh, Lillet, Noilly Prat and Suze). These make a tasty change to those normally found in Britain.

Clear, fruit flavoured eaux-de-vies are popular Alsace spirits, the same strength as gin or whisky but made from distilled fruits. They are delicious, and need to be drunk straight from the freezer.

Brightly coloured fruit liqueurs, either from Alsace

or Burgundy, are less than half the strength of eaux-de-vies. They are normally called 'Crème de–', followed by the fruit's name, and are rarely drunk on their own, but often mixed with white wine. The most famous is cassis, made from black-currants, which makes kir when mixed with white wine, or Kir Royale with champagne.

The basic flavours are given in the list below, so even if you don't recognise the brand, you can at least determine what its predominant taste will be.

France also offers a more exciting range of non-alcoholic drinks than Britain. These often have the words *'sans alcool'* prominently displayed on the label, and normally have their own clearly marked space in supermarkets. They come in a variety of flavours – *see* the list below – but particularly good are the aniseed (like pastis), mint, and herb ones.

Flavour	**Liqueur/Spirit**
Apricot	*Abricot*
Banana	*Banane*
Blackberry	*Mûre*
Blackcurrant	*Cassis*
Blue Plum	*Quetsch*
Cherry	*Kirsch/Cerise*
Chocolate	*Cacao*
Grapefruit	*Pamplemousse*
Juniper	*Genièvre (Genévrier)*
Peach	*Pêche*
Pear	*Poire* or *Poire Williams*
Peppermint	*Menthe*
Plum	*Mirabelle/Prune*
Prunes	*Pruneaux*
Raspberry	*Framboise*
Strawberry	*Fraise*
Wild Strawberry	*Fraise de Bois*

– INDEX –